STEEL SHIPS
AND
IRON MEN

by **Bruce Roberts and Ray Jones**

NORTHERN LIGHTHOUSES: New Brunswick to the Jersey Shore

SOUTHERN LIGHTHOUSES: From Chesapeake Bay to the Gulf of Mexico

AMERICAN COUNTRY STORES

STEEL SHIPS
AND
IRON MEN

A Tribute to World War II Fighting Ships and the Men Who Served on Them

Photographs by Bruce Roberts

Text by Ray Jones

The Globe Pequot Press

Chester, Connecticut

Credits for photographs not taken by author appear on page 148.

Library of Congress Cataloging-in-Publication Data

Roberts, Bruce, 1930–
    Steel ships and iron men: photographs/by Bruce Roberts ; text by Ray Jones.
       p.   cm.
    Includes index.
    ISBN 0–87106–244–5
    1. World War, 1939-1945—Navel operations, American–Pictorial works.
2. World War, 1939-1945—Navel operations, American. 3. Warships—United States—History—20th century—Pictorial works. 4. Warships—United States—History—20th century. I. Jones, Ray, 1948- . II. Title.
D773.R57 1991
940.54'5973—dc20   91-8568
                                                          CIP

Front cover: superstructure of the battleship *North Carolina*

Book design: Nancy Freeborn
Ship silhouettes: Duane Perrault
Cover design: Graphics Ink, Regine deToledo
Printed and bound in Hong Kong by Everbest Printing Co. Ltd.
First Edition/First Printing

To the pilots and crews of the torpedo bombers
launched by the carriers *Enterprise*, *Hornet*, and *Yorktown*
off Midway on the morning of June 4, 1942.
Their sacrifice changed the course of history.

JOHN CHARLES WALDRON
LIEUTENANT COMMANDER U.S. NAVY
1900 – 1942

DEDICATED SKIPPER OF TORPEDO SQUADRON 8
WHO ON 6.4.42, FROM HORNET CV–8, COURAGEOUSLY
LED 15 UNESCORTED OBSOLETE TBD'S, PILOTED
LARGELY BY USNR'S WHO HAD NEVER DROPPED
A TORPEDO EVEN IN PRACTICE, IN A RELENTLESS
ATTACK ON THE JAPANESE FLEET AT MIDWAY.
ALL BUT ONE OF THE 30 PILOTS AND CREW PERISHED.
HIS AND THEIR HEROISM DREW AWAY ENEMY ZEROS
FROM U.S. DIVE BOMBERS WHICH SANK 3 CARRIERS.

ELECTED TO CARRIER HALL OF FAME IN 1982.

Ghostly sentinels: Flanked by a pair of artillery pieces, a tank cuts a stark silhouette against the hull of the USS *Alabama* at Battleship Memorial Park in Mobile. At 35,000 tons, the battleship *Alabama* is a weighty reminder of sacrifices made more than half a century ago by millions of brave men and women. The *Alabama* and about thirty other fighting ships from World War II are on display in a variety of parks and memorials scattered across the country. Those who step aboard these steel veterans will learn firsthand of history's biggest and most desperate conflict.

Table of Contents

Old Glory snaps in a crisp breeze beside "Big Mamie," the USS *Massachusetts*.

Only a few survivors remain from the U.S. Navy's once vast World War II armada. Most succumbed to the scrapyard torch long ago, but some have found permanent homes in memorials and parks such as Patriots Point Naval and Maritime Museum in South Carolina. Pictured above are (left to right) the aircraft carrier *Yorktown*, submarine *Clamagore*, and destroyer *Laffey*.

Introduction

Half a century has passed since Japanese attack planes, red circles emblazoned on their wings, dropped down out of the morning sun over Honolulu. Ten presidents have served as chief executive of the United States since the first torpedo slammed into the battleship *Oklahoma,* dragging the United States into the biggest and bloodiest war in history. During the decades since bombs wrecked the *Nevada* and *Tennessee,* there have been Sputniks, Oswalds, Beatles, and Berlin Walls. Over the years since the *Arizona* exploded and sank, trapping 1,100 sailors in an oily tomb, Edsels and Studebakers have disappeared from highways to be replaced by Volkswagens, Hondas, Nissans, and Toyotas. Computers have become almost as common and indispensable as can openers in American homes, jet airlines have taken to the skies, and human beings have walked on the moon. Children born during the 1990s will stand as distant in time from the bombing of Pearl Harbor as the men and women who fought World War II stood from General Robert E. Lee's surrender at Appomattox Court House. Yet the war has not been—cannot be—forgotten.

World War II is remembered because of its enormous scope. It was truly a world war, fought on every continent except the Antarctic and in every sea and ocean on the planet. The war is remembered because, in large part, it shaped the world we live in today. More than half the nations on earth have come into existence since 1945, most of them as a result of political and economic forces set in motion by the Allied victory. The war is remembered because it was a pivotal experience for all mankind, a moment when civilization itself seemed about to disintegrate. It serves as a signpost warning us away from the mistakes of the past.

World War II continues to fascinate people today, more than fifty years after it began. It remains a favorite setting for movies and novels. Television serials about the war attract and entertain large audiences. Middle-aged baby boomers—by definition, born after the war ended— and their children seem just as interested in D-Day, Anzio, and Iwo Jima as their parents and grandparents. And why not? The war was a time of action, a time filled with blitzkriegs, V-2 rockets, fighter aces, concrete pillboxes, and hard-charging Marines, a time of thundering battleships and fast carriers, a time of steel ships and iron men.

Damage control crews fight fires aboard the *Yorktown* after the carrier was attacked by Japanese dive bombers and torpedo planes during the Battle of Midway, June 3-6, 1942.

Struck by torpedoes, the *Yorktown* lists sharply to port. Soon afterward, the crew was ordered to abandon ship.

A Floating Legend

On May 8, 1942, Japanese pilots returning from a successful strike against a U.S. Navy task force in the Coral Sea unwittingly gave birth to a cherished American legend. The exuberant airmen told their commanders they had sunk the famed aircraft carrier *Yorktown.* They were mistaken.

Much of what the Imperial Navy pilots reported that day was true. A swarm of seventy attack planes had pounded the *Yorktown* and an older carrier, *Lexington,* leaving them engulfed in flame. Columns of dense, black smoke rolled skyward from the decks of the two ships. There could have been little doubt that both had been destroyed.

However, the U. S. Navy lost only one carrier in the battle, when a series of tremendous internal explosions tore apart the "Lady Lex." Damage control crews on the *Yorktown* managed to beat back the flames and save their ship from a similar fate. Battered but not beaten, the big flattop was soon back in fighting trim and racing northward on a 5,000-mile odyssey destined to end less than a month later near the strategic island of Midway

Pilots in the first wave of Japanese planes attacking the American fleet off Midway did not expect to encounter the *Yorktown,* a ship supposedly rusting at the bottom of the Coral Sea. They must have thought they were diving down on some other carrier, perhaps the *Enterprise* or the *Hornet.* Whatever its identity, they hit the mystery ship hard, placing three heavy bombs on the flight deck. Then, returning to their own fleet, they reported the sinking of an American aircraft carrier. Again their report was in error.

Once more the crew of the *Yorktown* worked miracles, dousing flames and patching the punctured deck. By the time a second wave of

Sailors clear away debris from a bomb explosion that reached deep into the bowels of the *Yorktown* during the Battle of Coral Sea, May 8, 1942. The *Yorktown* survived this battering, only to be sunk less than a month later off Midway.

Japanese warplanes closed in, little more than two hours later, the *Yorktown* had the outward appearance of an undamaged ship. The attacking pilots found it impossible to believe this was the same vessel their dive-bombers had blasted earlier in the day. Nonetheless, they swooped down and put two torpedoes into the port side of the carrier. The Japanese had "sunk" the *Yorktown* yet again.

This time, the carrier's wounds were truly grievous. The exploding torpedoes seemed to lift the huge ship out of the water, bringing engines to a dead stop and creating a list so severe that crewmen could scarcely stand upright on the flight deck. Soon the crew was forced to abandon the ship they knew affectionately as "Waltzing Matilda." But still the stubborn carrier did not sink.

For many hours this empty shell of a fighting ship drifted with no human hand at the helm to steer. Then salvage crews were ordered aboard to try, one more time, to save the still smouldering *Yorktown*. They had begun to think they might succeed, when two days after the battle, the carrier lined up in the periscope crosshairs of the Japanese submarine *I-168*. The enemy sub pumped two more torpedoes into the ship's weakened sides. A few hours later, the *Yorktown* rolled over and sank in waters more than two miles deep.

This was not the end of the *Yorktown* saga. The Navy already had under construction a whole new fleet of powerful *Essex*-class carriers. One of these was honored with a name made legendary not only by General Washington's decisive Revolutionary War victory, but also in the Coral Sea and at Midway. By the middle of 1943, the Japanese were again forced to battle the carrier *Yorktown*.

Unsinkable Ships

Although made the target of repeated bomb and torpedo attacks and clawed by suicide planes off Okinawa, the new carrier lived up to its unsinkable name. Today, the *Yorktown* numbers among the few survivors remaining from all the thousands of ships that served in the U.S. Navy and armed merchant marine during World War II. Nearly all of that once vast fleet has vanished. Axis shells, bombs, and torpedoes took a heavy toll on ships during the war. Others perished in wrecks and hurricanes during the nearly half century since the war's end. Some were sunk intentionally during nuclear bomb tests or by Navy gunners taking target practice. But most succumbed in a more ignominious fashion—to the scrapyard torch.

Surprisingly, a handful of World War II veterans—the battleships *New Jersey, Iowa, Wisconsin,* and *Missouri,* all recommissioned during the 1980s—remain on duty with the U.S. Navy. But the *Yorktown* is no longer counted among the Navy's active warships. Permanently berthed

at Patriots Point near Charleston, South Carolina, this 42,000-ton legend serves as a maritime museum and memorial to the ships and sailors who fought and won the naval battles of World War II.

The *Yorktown* is part of an impressive and varied memorial fleet of more than thirty fighting ships, including fast carriers, battleships, destroyers, submarines, PT-boats, Liberty-type cargo ships, and even a minesweeper. The memorial fleet is scattered. A majority of its vessels—almost half of them submarines—are located in ports and rivers along the U.S. East and Gulf coasts. Others can be found in California and Hawaii, or in states such as Ohio, Wisconsin, and Oklahoma, where cornfields are a far more common sight than expanses of salt water.

Wherever the memorial vessels are found, they are a source of tremendous pride. Often, much of the money needed to preserve the ships has been raised locally. The cost of maintaining a rust-prone steel ship as big as a city skyscraper—the *Yorktown* is almost 900 feet long—can run to millions of dollars annually. But the thousands of wide-eyed visitors who tour the old fighting ships every week would agree that the money is well spent. So would the thousands of veterans who return each year for shipboard reunions.

These venerable ships and submarines, together with the sailors who served aboard them and similar vessels, are the subject of this book. Intended as a guide to the nation's World War II ship memorials, the book describes the World War II ships, submarines, and other vessels open to the public and tells some of their war stories. To encourage readers to visit these living history exhibits, each of them an educational experience of rare value, travel information is included. Through anecdotes and narratives drawn from veterans and their families, the book also attempts to convey a sense of what it was like to serve as a sailor in World War II.

The hangar deck of the second *Yorktown*, launched after the sinking of its predecessor, is a treasure trove of wartime memories. Visitors usually begin their tours of the big carrier on this exciting deck.

Postcard from Pearl

On December 8, 1937, George McGowan signed his Navy enlistment papers and slung a duffle bag over his shoulder. He was eighteen at the time, from a small southern town, and, like every other Navy recruit, wanted to see the world. But after serving four years, the last few months of that time aboard the *Enterprise,* one of the Navy's spanking new fast carriers, McGowan figured he had seen enough. Having decided not to reenlist, he made plans to return to his family's modest home in Ensley, Alabama. Maybe he would use the technical skills he had learned in the Navy to help him get a good job in one of the huge steel mills near Ensley. He counted the days. Officially, he was scheduled to become a civilian again on December 7, 1941.

Things did not work out as McGowan had hoped. The *Enterprise* was due to arrive at Pearl Harbor by Sunday, December 7, in plenty of time for McGowan to spend his last day as a sailor in Honolulu. But there were unexpected delays. When December 7 dawned, the ship was still far out at sea. As the day progressed, a rash of wild, unbelievable rumors began to spread among the *Enterprise* enlisted men. Trouble at Pearl. Bombers. Torpedo planes. A plane from the *Enterprise* shot down.

Much later, when McGowan's carrier finally reached Pearl Harbor, the truth of the rumors became all too shockingly apparent. Wherever McGowan and the other men of the *Enterprise* looked, ruined ships lay half submerged in the harbor's shallow waters. Some had capsized, their hulls crushed like empty cans. Twisted hulks lined the once-mighty battleship row. Smoke still billowed from some of the wrecks. Fires still burned on shore as well. It was incredible, astounding. The U.S. Navy's Pacific Headquarters had been all but destroyed. The refuge of Pearl Harbor had been shattered, along with the lives and dreams of a great many people.

In Alabama, McGowan's family and friends waited anxiously for word of him. They had expected any day to be sharing dinner and gossip with him and listening to his sea stories. Now they did not even know if he was alive. His mother cried. His sister, who had recently fallen in love with a steelworker, did not cry, but wondered whether her brother would make it home in time for her wedding.

Navy censors provided sailors with postcards like the one shown below, which was mailed from Honolulu only a few days after the bombing of Pearl Harbor. George McGowan's family in Alabama knew this card portended a radical change in plans for him. His original date of discharge from the Navy was December 7, 1941.

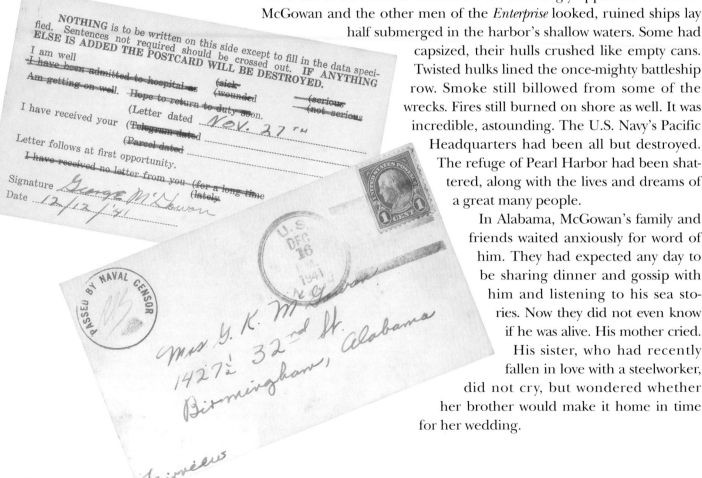

At last a postcard arrived from the Pacific. Printed by military censors, it was designed to reveal as little information as possible. The card said, "I am" and then gave the sender the option of checking boxes indicating "well," "sick," etc. Nonetheless, the card made its point loud and clear. George was "well," at least for the moment. And, written between the printed lines—in the invisible ink of human understanding—was another message. George would not be coming home for a very long time.

A Fishing Permit

The bombing of Pearl Harbor plunged Americans headlong into a war very different from any that had been fought before. This was partly because of advances in the technology of warfare—air strength would be a vital consideration in practically every battle. But it was also true because of geography. Every child who owns a globe knows that one side of our planet is blue. More than 5,000 miles of open ocean, broken only by a few tiny atolls and volcanic islands, separate San Francisco and Tokyo. Throughout much of American history, the broad Pacific had provided the nation with a deep sense of security, separating it from the dangers of the Orient, just as the Atlantic insulated the country from the endless turmoil of Europe.

After the attack on Pearl Harbor, Americans began to take a very different view of the Pacific. To an enemy such as Japan, with its powerful navy, the ocean was not an obstacle; it was, instead, an open highway that might very well be used for invasion. The bright blue expanses that had once shielded America had now turned dark and threatening. As a consequence, ships became the nation's most prized possessions, and sailors stood tall in the minds of every American. The U.S. Navy became what the ocean had been before the attack, a protecting wall.

What most Americans did not know, however, though many must have suspected, was that their defensive wall was in danger of crumbling. With their very first blow, the Japanese had come dangerously close to breaching it. They had caught America unprepared, off balance. For defense of the west coast, the U.S. Navy could no longer rely on its fleet of battleships, crippled at Pearl Harbor, or its carriers, heavily outnumbered by the Japanese. During the first queasy months of war, America's defense depended largely on a thin picket line of submarines.

"It was easy enough to see that we had gotten ourselves into a Navy war," said Jack Killough, a submarine veteran. In 1941, Killough served on the U.S. submarine *Permit,* stationed in the Philippines. (Later in the war he served on the USS *Drum,* now on memorial display in Mobile, Alabama.)

"We saw the war getting ready to start," said Killough. "A lot of bitter things had passed between us and the Japanese, but, to tell the truth, most of us didn't think war was coming. Maybe we should have, though. You see, we had already fought with the Japanese."

Only half joking, Killough told the story of his first "battle." It happened, he said, long before the war officially started. "It was on a public beach in China. We [a group of American sailors on liberty] got in an argument with some Japanese airmen. One of them was trying to tell us how they were the Emperor's chosen few and how the Emperor was God and how they were going to conquer the world for him. Well, we didn't want to listen to any of that, and as it ended up, we beat them up. We won that fight, all right. We had the advantage because there were a lot more of us and we were a lot drunker."

On December 8, 1941, Killough's submarine, the *Permit* (SS-178), was in Manila Harbor for repair on one of its engines. Killough, an engineman, had gone into town that day to see a movie. After he returned to the *Permit,* he fell asleep, but he was soon awakened by an urgent message from a nearby submarine tender: JAPAN HAS COMMENCED HOSTILITIES. GO TO WAR PLAN 46.

"I figured, okay, so we are at war," said Killough. "But what the hell is War Plan 46?"

Killough and his fellow submarine sailors waited anxiously for their captain, who had been ashore when the message came. The skipper returned a short while later, and they learned the meaning of the cryptic command, "Go to War Plan 46." It was an order to strip their vessel of all unnecessary gear and be prepared for immediate action.

"That was not as easy for us as for some of the others [i.e., Navy fighting ships]. A war had just started, and there we were with pieces of our engine scattered all over the deck."

Nonetheless, the crew of the *Permit* soon had their engine back together and their submarine readied for combat. "We were all excited," said Killough. "It wasn't as if we wanted to go to war, but we were in the Navy, you see. Before Pearl Harbor, it

During the first desperate months of war, the Navy held back the Japanese with a thin picket line of submarines such as the USS *Drum*, shown below in Mobile. Submariner Jack Killough served first on the *Permit* and later on the *Drum*.

was like having a fishing pole and plenty of bait but no license. And now that message had told us it was all right to go fishing."

Within days the *Permit* was stalking the fleet sent by the Japanese to support their invasion of Luzon, the largest island in the Philippine chain. "Finally, we tangled with a Japanese destroyer. It was a one-sided fight, though, and he just brushed us aside as if we were some sort of water bug. We fired two torpedoes out of the stern tubes but got no hits. He just brushed them aside."

Even if the torpedoes had hit the destroyer, it may have made no difference. During the early part of the war, U.S. Navy torpedoes worked very poorly. The trigger mechanism in their explosive heads tended to jam so that the torpedoes bounced harmlessly off their targets. "There were plenty of things that didn't work the way they were supposed to. We had never done any of this before, you see, never fired a torpedo at an enemy ship."

While the *Permit*'s first attack of the war fizzled, the Japanese response proved almost fatal to the submarine crew. "They depth-charged us, and a flying boat tried to get us with a 500-pound bomb. The bomb missed but still did quite a bit of damage. Hearing that thing go off was like being sealed in a steel drum and having somebody drop a battleship anchor on it."

The battered *Permit* limped back to Manila. Because of the threat of air attacks, repairs could only be made at night. To avoid the Japanese bombers, the submarine spent the daylight hours submerged, resting on the shallow harbor bottom. During the day, temperature and humidity inside the *Permit* soared so that many members of the crew fell ill with heat exhaustion. "When we finally had her patched up enough to go to sea, we got the hell out of there."

Later, the *Permit* rescued the crew of one of the four PT-boats that had taken General Douglas MacArthur and his family off Corregidor. "Their boat had engine trouble during MacArthur's run out of the Philippines. Naturally, they made room for MacArthur and his people on the other boats, but some of the crew had to be left behind. They just waved goodbye and left those guys on a small island to do the Robinson Crusoe thing. So they were plenty happy to see us."

Working its way out of the Philippines, the *Permit* shifted its base of operations to Java, in the Dutch East Indies (now Indonesia). "But the Japanese still bombed us almost every day. One day there was a Dutch submarine, the *K-13*, tied up to the dock across from us. When the air raid started, the *K-13* threw off her lines and tried to submerge right there beside the dock, but the Japanese put a bomb square on top of her. We never saw any of the *K-13*'s crew again. It was a terrible thing to consider, but we figured, sooner or later, something like that would happen to us too. You just did your job and tried not to think too much about it all."

FACES ON A WALL

On the morning of June 4, 1942, Lt. Commander John C. Waldron stood in the flight ready room of the carrier *Hornet* giving final instructions to his young, inexperienced torpedo pilots before flying off with them into one of history's most decisive naval battles. His manner was much like that of a football coach whipping up the spirits of his players before a big game. "If there is only one plane left to make a final run-in," said Waldron, "I want that man to go in and get a hit."

Then, in a more subdued tone, as if he realized these last words had been prophetic, Waldron added, "May God be with us all."

Located in a far, out-of-the-way corner on the hangar deck of the carrier *Yorktown* at Patriots Point is a remarkable display. It consists mostly of grainy, black-and-white photographs revealing the faces of more than fifty young men, all dead for half a century now. The faces are at once shockingly youthful and hauntingly familiar. We've seen faces like these on street corners and campuses, in garages and the young men's clothing sections of department stores. There are Lieutenant Patrick Hayes, Lieutenant JG (junior grade) Curtis Howard, and Machinist John Hass, all with the bright smiles and the self-assurance one might expect of Ivy League college boys. There is Ensign Oswald Powers with his impish grin and hat cocked to one side; Ensign David Roche, who, without a doubt, suffered the nickname "Roach"; Ensign William Evans, who has his sleeves rolled up, and might have been a Texas cowboy; Ensign Carl Osberg, a prankster whose face and name suggest a German heritage; and Ensign Flourenoy Hodges, whose first name must have made him the butt of many painful jokes. There is John Cole, whose very serious expression indicates worry, maybe about his folks, or a girl back home. Probably it was a girl; Cole looks like a heartbreaker, and the wall behind him in the picture, marked off line-up-style in feet and inches, shows he stood more than 2 inches over 6 feet tall. There is Leo Perry, who is losing his hair, and William Phillips, who has plenty of hair. John Bates is baby-faced, almost too pretty. John Blundell is not so pretty. The best word to describe Ensign William Creamer is average, an ordinary young man. But his name is suggestive. It is easy to imagine his friends sending him roaring down the deck of his carrier and off into the crucial Battle of Midway with shouts of "Cream 'em, Bill!"

Bill Creamer did not "cream" the enemy on that day—June 4, a Thursday. Neither did the other men whose faces cover the wall of the

Yorktown's Midway exhibit. What they did, instead, was launch a series of suicidal and utterly unsuccessful torpedo runs on the Japanese carriers steaming toward Midway Island. Not one of them damaged an enemy vessel. Not one of them survived the attack. But the importance of what they did, of their sacrifice, is beyond measure.

Japanese Admiral Yamamoto and his trusted fleet commander Nagumo had known from the beginning that strength in the air would decide the outcome of any war with the United States. In fact, their seemingly brilliant victory at Pearl Harbor had bitterly disappointed them; they had dealt the Americans a heavy blow but had sunk no carriers. So, a few months later, they set in motion a grand scheme designed to draw the U.S. carriers into a final, annihilating battle. Late in May 1942, Yamamoto and Nagumo led an enormous fleet out into the Pacific. Their immediate objective was the American-held island of Midway, but their real purpose was the destruction of the U. S. carrier fleet.

Admiral Chester Nimitz, the U.S. Navy's Pacific commander, reacted in much the way Yamamoto had hoped. He committed three of his finest carriers to the defense of Midway. The *Enterprise* and *Hornet* were stationed to the north and east of the island. The *Yorktown,* still bearing the.battle scars brought back from the Coral Sea, stood close by.

Unknown to the Japanese, Nimitz carried a secret advantage into the battle. American intelligence forces had broken the Japanese naval code. Messages flashing back and forth between members of the Imperial high command had been intercepted and decoded by U.S. cryptographers; these messages indicated an imminent attack on Midway. Since he knew his enemy's intentions, Nimitz resolved to turn the tables on them and bushwhack their carriers. While the Japanese were sending waves of bombers to pulverize defensive positions on Midway, Nimitz ordered his fleet commanders, vice admirals Jack Fletcher and Raymond Spruance, to launch an all-out air assault on the enemy fleet.

Nimtitz's carefully mapped-out strategy was sound, but as often happens in war, things did not go according to plan. The American attack was badly organized, almost haphazard. Except for an extraordinary coincidence and the even more extraordinary bravery of a few dozen young airmen, it might have fizzled all together.

In order to place maximum pressure on the Japanese fleet and penetrate its formidable antiaircraft and fighter defenses, the American torpedo and dive-bomber squadrons needed to launch coordinated attacks. To do this, they had to arrive over the enemy fleet simultaneously, along with their fighter escorts. They did not.

An aircraft carrier, such as the 41,300-ton Japanese flagship *Akagi,* is a huge target, but the immensity of the Pacific reduces its relative scale to that of a single grain of sand in a square mile of desert. During the long and difficult search for the *Akagi* and other Japanese carriers, the various squadrons from the *Hornet, Enterprise,* and *Yorktown* became widely separated. Some got lost, ran low on fuel, and had to turn back. The torpedo planes finally located the enemy, but to their dismay, found that they had lost contact with both the dive-bombers and their own fighter escorts. Waldron and the other torpedo squadron leaders knew there was no time to regroup, in fact, not a split second to waste. Without a moment's hesitation, Waldron formed the *Hornet*'s squadron into a wedge-shaped formation, and pointing this spearhead at the enemy carriers, gave the order to attack.

It was hopeless. With no fighter cover, the lumbering torpedo planes were jumped from left, right, and rear by fire-spitting Japanese Zeros. Antiaircraft fire knocked off wings and turned fuselages into torches. Each in its turn, the torpedo squadrons were treated to the same deadly reception. Only a few planes got close enough to launch their torpedoes, and only one scored a hit. Of the forty-one torpedo planes sent aloft by the American carriers that day, four returned safely to the *Enterprise,* two to the *Yorktown,* and none to the *Hornet.* The scores of airmen who died, Waldron among them, struck the water without knowing the outcome of the battle, let alone that of the war. Those who had time to think before the blackness closed over them must have feared the worst.

Having destroyed or driven off wave after wave of attackers, sailors on the Japanese ships had reason to think victory was close at hand. But any elation they felt was short-lived. Only a minute or so after the last

Carrier-launched Dauntless dive bombers cruise at 16,000 feet on their way to hit the Japanese at Lae-Salamava, March 10, 1942.

shattered torpedo plane fell into the ocean, crewmen on the *Akagi,* *Kaga,* and *Soryu* heard the scream of plunging dive-bombers. Moments later all three carriers erupted in smoke and flame.

In one of the war's most fateful coincidences, the Navy dive-bomber squadrons had arrived at just the right instant. The protective umbrella over the Japanese fleet had collapsed when scores of Zeros swooped down to wave level to dispatch the hapless American torpedo planes. This left no fighters overhead to stop the dive-bombers. Later that day, dive-bombers also blasted a fourth Japanese carrier, the *Hiryu.* All four of the bombed carriers eventually sank. The heart of the Japanese fleet had been destroyed, and the Imperial Navy would never recover from the blow.

An increasing variety of board games allow armchair warriors to simulate some of history's greatest battles. If they wish, players may general the German divisions at Stalingrad, lead the Continental Army at Yorktown, or stand in Wellington's shoes at Waterloo. Sometimes the games produce surprising results. Occasionally, Napoleon wins at Waterloo, or Cornwallis crushes Washington in Virginia. But the verdict in most of these recreated battles is the same as the one originally handed down by history—General Lee usually retreats from Gettysburg, just as he did in 1863. But there is one notable exception. Players report that the odds are so heavily stacked in favor of the Japanese that the American side almost never wins the Battle of Midway.

The USS *Arizona* Memorial at Pearl Harbor

Battleship Row comes under attack by Japanese aircraft on December 7, 1941. The paired ships are (from top left) *Nevada* and *Arizona*, *Tennessee* and *West Virginia*, *Maryland* and *Oklahoma*. A Japanese pilot took this dramatic photograph.

The *Arizona* explodes and burns after being hit repeatedly by bombs and torpedoes.

The stunning news of the Pearl Harbor bombing no doubt confronted many, some perhaps in this fashion, as they entered the officers' wardroom. This well-set table can be seen on the destroyer *Kidd* at Baton Rouge, Louisiana.

With their light, plywood hulls, the relatively inexpensive PT boats were considered "expendable" by some naval planners. Striking from island chains throughout the Pacific, the PTs relentlessly harassed Japanese supply fleets.

CHAPTER ONE

MOSQUITO SQUADRONS

"We were light, fast, and had a sting," said PT-boat Motor Machinist Robert Benson. "That's why they called us mosquito boats."

Outgunned during the early months of the war, the U. S. Navy was forced to rely on the hit-and-run tactics of its smaller, faster vessels to hold back the rising tide of Japanese sea power. The smallest and fastest of them all were the Navy's new PT (Patrol Torpedo) boats. An innovative naval weapon, the PT-boat had a wooden hull, usually between 77 and 80 feet in length, and carried a crew of only ten. But racing through the waves at 40 knots (46 mph) or more, a PT could pack a fearsome punch with its four torpedoes.

"We scared the business out of them," said Benson. "The Japanese had never seen anything like us."

To keep Japanese battle fleets and convoys off balance, the Navy sent swarms of PTs into the island chains of the South Pacific. During daylight hours, the tiny, though astonishingly aggressive, attack boats lurked in remote lagoons or along the banks of rivers where the spreading limbs of giant trees provided camouflage. "We had to hide during the day," said Benson. "The enemy would send out hundreds of planes looking for us. Were we small, but we were a tremendous annoyance to them, like a stinging insect, and they wanted to slap us."

At night the PTs emerged from their hiding places and went into action. "Usually, by the time it was dark, we'd be out on station. We'd work our way into position and wait for the Tokyo Express [Japanese convoys]. You might sit out there the whole night and never see or do a damn thing. Then on the next night they would show up, and off you'd go to throw a couple of fish [torpedoes] at them."

Benson's most thrilling and dangerous night missions came in the Solomon Islands aboard PT-65. (Serving in the same squadron with Benson was the young future president John Fitzgerald Kennedy, commander of the now famous PT-109.) "Our skipper in the Solomons was Lieutenant Ward Coe, and he despised wasting torpedoes. He hated to miss, so we'd get in as close as 500 or 600 yards before we'd throw our fish."

The zigzagging PTs were so maneuverable, they made the big guns on the Japanese warships practically useless. "By the time the enemy gunners had aimed and fired we were somewhere else, or at least we hoped we were. But they fired away at us anyway with 5-inchers, 3-inchers, antiaircraft, whatever they happened to have on deck. They used rifles and machine guns too; I've still got a hole in my arm from a 9mm slug."

The PTs blazed back with their own 20mm and 40mm guns and .50-caliber machine guns. "A lot of the stuff we used was homemade, converted from old field guns or whatever we could get our hands on."

The mission of the PTs was to harass the enemy. They were not expected to stand and "slug it out" with warships, which nearly always had overwhelmingly superior fire power. "We would sling our fish at them and get out of there as fast as we could. But that was not always so easy. The Japanese tin cans [destroyers] were fast, and they would chase us. When we couldn't outrun them, we would drop a couple of depth charges in our wake. If one of those went off under a destroyer, it could pop rivets out of the hull; they could damn near lose the bottom right out of their boat."

Following a torpedo run, enemy warships often combed the dark seas for hours searching for the pesky PTs that were tormenting their fleet. They were sometimes assisted in their hunt by a glowing trail of phosphorescent seawater left by a PT's churning propellers. "Unless we were careful, they could follow that glow right to us. So we would cut our engines and drift until they stopped looking for us."

More often than not, the mosquito boats escaped their pursuers to return night after night and send their torpedoes slashing through the water toward Japanese destroyers and freighters. By harassing convoys and helping to squeeze off the flow of supplies to enemy land forces, the PTs played a role similar to that of submarines. "We made the enemy transports so nervous that they no longer stopped to unload their cargo. They just dumped it overboard and let it drift ashore. So we would move around out there and shoot up their supplies."

Because of their small size, the PTs themselves made a poor target for the torpedoes of other vessels, including submarines. Benson's boat was among the few PTs known to have engaged an enemy submarine. "As soon as we saw the sub, we started throwing gunfire at it. We weren't able to sink it, but we did drive it into a minefield. A few minutes later we saw a flash and heard an explosion. As far as we knew, that was the end of the sub."

Despite their speed and the advantage of being a small target, the PTs and their daring crews often paid a heavy price for the damage they inflicted. Although the fast-moving PTs could keep enemy gunners guessing, usually a single shell was enough to sink them. Their wooden hulls could easily be holed, even by machine-gun bullets. Dozens of PTs were lost, many without a trace of boat or crew.

"The way the admirals saw it, if they lost a PT, they hadn't lost that much—ten guys and a wooden boat," said Benson. The U.S. Navy paid $135,000 for the hulls of PT-boats. That compared very favorably with the millions spent on big, steel-hulled warships. A battleship might take months or even years to build; and if such a ship were sunk, it would likely drag hundreds of men to their deaths. So the PTs were seen as a comparatively economical way to fight the war.

A movie made in 1944 about PT-boat action in the Pacific carried the poignant title *They Were Expendable*. The title mirrors the opinions of naval experts both during and after World War II; in their view, the PTs were, in fact, highly expendable, and therein lay their extraordinary value to the U.S. war effort.

But PT-boat commanders and crewman, who were known widely as mavericks, typically held a different view of the situation. Veterans who served on the mosquito boats sometimes put it this way: "They may have thought we were expendable. We didn't."

A single enemy shell could easily shatter their wooden hulls, but the PT boats were fast and maneuverable and packed a knockout punch with their torpedoes. The PT below is housed in a building at Battleship Cove in Fall River, Massachusetts.

BOSTON, MASSACHUSETTS

USS *Cassin Young* (DD793)

Classification:	Destroyer, Fletcher class
Sister Ships:	*The Sullivans* (DD537), *Kidd* (DD661)
Crew:	19 officers, 306 enlisted men
Length:	376 feet 6 inches
Beam:	39 feet 8 inches
Displacement:	2,050 tons (3,035 when fully loaded for combat)
Engines:	4 boilers, 2 electric-geared turbines, 3 generators
Power:	36 knots (41 mph) maximum speed
Armament:	Five 5" dual purpose guns Ten 40mm antiaircraft guns Seven 20mm antiaircraft guns Ten 21" torpedo tubes in two quintuple banks Six depth charge projectors (K-guns) Two depth charge tracks
Wartime Achievements:	Earned four Battle Stars, Navy Unit Commendation, Philippine Liberation Medal, and World War II Victory Medal

The destroyer USS *Cassin Young,* one of the Navy's workhorse ships, bears the name of a Navy captain who was awarded the Medal of Honor for his heroic actions in saving the repair ship *Vestal* and rescuing survivors from the *Arizona* on December 7, 1941, at Pearl Harbor and who was posthumously awarded the Navy Cross for his gallantry on the night of November 12, 1942, during the Battle of Guadalcanal. Built by Bethlehem Steel Corporation at San Pedro, California, the USS *Cassin Young* was commissioned on December 31, 1943.

The *Cassin Young* spent her entire World War II career with the Pacific Fleet, performing such duties as escorting other ships, participating in shore bombardments, rescuing downed airmen and survivors from stricken ships, and serving as picket and mail ship. Her first taste of combat came in April 1944 when she helped attack Japanese strong-holds in the Caroline Islands.

In June 1944 the *Cassin Young* escorted the amphibious forces that invaded Saipan, Tinian, and Guam, and in July she joined Task Group 38.3 assigned to escort several aircraft carriers. From October 23 to 27, 1944, the destroyer participated in the Battle for Leyte Gulf, rescuing more than 120 survivors from the aircraft carrier *Princeton* and providing escort for the remaining carriers. The *Cassin Young* continued on escort duty to help protect the carriers that provided air cover for the American troops in the Philippines.

In January 1945 the destroyer cruised with the other ships in her task force to the waters off Formosa, Indochina, and the southern coast of China in preparation for the invasions of Iwo Jima and Okinawa. During February and March, the *Cassin Young* provided support for the Marine landings on Iwo Jima and bombarded Japanese strongholds on Okinawa.

Reassigned to Task Force 54 for D-Day at Okinawa (April 1, 1945), the destroyer escorted assault craft and provided shore bombardment. The *Cassin Young* also served as a radar picket ship to provide the other ships in the fleet with early warning of enemy air attacks. As a picket ship, one of the most dangerous wartime assignments, the destroyer

Doing about 15 knots, the destroyer *Cassin Young* leaves California and heads for the open Pacific. The irregular stripes on the hull are for camouflage.

Survivors from the aircraft carrier *Princeton* jump from a lifeboat and swim toward the rescuing *Cassin Young*. The *Princeton* went down during the Battle of Leyte Gulf, October 23-27, 1944.

endured numerous kamikaze attacks, including a mass assault on April 6 when 355 Japanese kamikazes and 341 bombers hit and sank two of the destroyers serving with the *Cassin Young*. Six days later, during another massive air attack, the destroyer shot down six kamikazes, but one hit the ship's mast and exploded, killing one crewman and injuring fifty-nine others.

On July 30 a single kamikaze crashed into the *Cassin Young*'s main deck near the forward smokestack, setting off a tremendous explosion that killed twenty-two of the crew and injured forty-five. The ship lost power with the explosion, but the crew was able to contain the damage and restore power in one engine within twenty minutes. The destroyer received the Navy Unit Commendation for her determined service and gallantry on the Okinawa radar picket line.

At the end of World War II, the *Cassin Young* returned to California, where she was decommissioned by the Navy and placed in the reserve fleet. The outbreak of the Korean War brought the *Cassin Young* back to active duty in the Atlantic and Mediterranean. In 1952 she was modernized in a major overhaul at the Charlestown Navy Yard in Boston. In 1954 the *Cassin Young* patrolled the waters off Korea, and from 1955 to 1959 she served with four deployments in the Atlantic and Caribbean.

The Navy decommissioned the destroyer again on April 29, 1960, assigning her to the mothball fleet at Norfolk. Acquired by the National Park Service in 1978 and restored to her late-1950s condition, the *Cassin Young* has been open to the public since 1981.

The USS *Cassin Young* is open for tours at Boston National Historical Park at the old Charlestown Navy Yard off U.S. 1 (just north of the intersection of Interstate 93 and U.S. 1). The park also includes the preserved frigate USS *Constitution*.

FALL RIVER, MASSACHUSETTS

USS *Massachusetts* (BB59)

Classification:	Battleship, South Dakota class
Sister Ships:	*South Dakota* (BB57), *Indiana* (BB58), *Alabama* (BB60)
Crew:	2,300 to 2,500 officers and enlisted men
Length:	680 feet 10 inches
Beam:	108 feet 2 inches
Displacement:	35,000 tons (46,000 to 51,000 tons when fully loaded for combat)
Engines:	4 engine rooms, each with 2 boilers and 2 turbines
Power:	130,000 HP maximum, 30 knots (35 mph) maximum speed
Armament:	Nine 16" guns Twenty 5" guns Eighteen 40mm antiaircraft guns in quad mounts Thirty-five 20mm antiaircraft guns Three aircraft Two launching catapults
Wartime Achievements:	Earned eleven Battle Stars and is credited with firing both the first (on November 8, 1942, at Casablanca) and the last (on August 9, 1945, at Honshu) American 16-inch shells fired during the war
Nickname:	"Big Mamie"

Built by the Bethlehem Steel Company in Quincy, Massachusetts, the USS *Massachusetts* was commissioned on May 12, 1942. After completing her shakedown training along the East Coast, the battleship steamed across the Atlantic to join the Western Naval Task Force for the invasion of North Africa, where she served as the flagship for Admiral H. Kent Hewitt.

On November 8, 1942, she dueled with the Vichy French battleship *Jean Bart* being fitted out at Casablanca. (The Vichy regime of France collaborated with Nazi Germany during the early portion of the war.) While still tied to the dock at Casablanca, the enemy ship opened fire with her 15-inch guns, but the *Massachusetts* quickly overpowered the *Jean Bart* with her 16-inch shells (the first fired by an American ship during the war) and sank the two French destroyers that had joined in the battle. The battleship also bombarded French strongholds on shore, including an ammunition dump. After the French forces agreed to a cease-fire, the *Massachusetts* returned to the East Coast to prepare for duty in the Pacific.

The battleship arrived at Nouméa, in New Caledonia, on March 4,

The USS *Massachusetts* lies at its permanent berth in Fall River, Massachusetts. Outlined by a July sunset, the battleship's superstructure rivals that of the bridge in the background.

1943. For the next several months she guarded convoy lanes and provided support for U.S. operations in the Solomon Islands. From November 19 to 21, 1943, the *Massachusetts* worked with a carrier group striking enemy sites in the Gilbert Islands.

The *Massachusetts* participated in shore bombardments on Kwajalein on January 30, 1944, and provided cover for U.S. troop landings there on February 1. She worked with a carrier group in the assault on Truk (February 17, 1944) and later helped fight off heavy enemy air attacks while her task force raided Saipan, Tinian, and Guam.

In late March and early April 1944, the battleship provided support for the attack on the Caroline Islands and the invasion of Hollandia. After participating in a second assault on Truk and shelling Ponape, the *Massachusetts* withdrew to the naval yard at Puget Sound for a major overhaul.

Returning to Pearl Harbor in July 1944, the battleship rejoined the Pacific Fleet in time to support U.S. landings at Leyte Gulf. In October 1944 the *Massachusetts* participated in the attacks on Okinawa and Formosa and provided cover for the other ships in her task force during the Battle of Leyte Gulf.

After a brief stopover at Ulithi, the battleship served in a task force assaulting Manila (December 14, 1944) and Formosa (December 30, 1944–January 23, 1945). Her next assignment took the *Massachusetts* into the South China Sea to disrupt enemy shipping between Saigon and Hong Kong.

As part of the Fifth Fleet during February and March 1945, the battleship guarded aircraft carriers during raids on Honshu, Iwo Jima, and Okinawa. In April 1945 she bombarded enemy positions in the Ryukyus, and in July 1945 the battleship joined the Third Fleet for the final assault on Japan. The *Massachusetts* shelled major enemy industrial centers on Honshu during July and August, and it was during her bombardment of Kamaishi on August 9, 1945, that she fired what is thought to be the last American 16-inch shell fired during the war.

The *Massachusetts* returned to Puget Sound when the war ended and participated in operations off the California coast until she was sent to Hampton Roads, Virginia, in April 1946. After earning eleven battle stars for her outstanding wartime service, the *Massachusetts* was decommissioned on March 27, 1947, and place in the Atlantic Reserve Fleet at Norfolk, Virginia. The *Massachusetts* Memorial Committee petitioned the Navy to give them possession of the ship as a memorial, and the battleship was transferred to them on June 8, 1965. The *Massachusetts* was opened to the public at her permanent berth at Fall River, Massachusetts, on August 14, 1965.

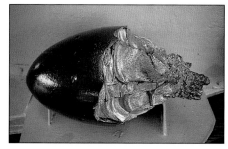

On November 8, 1942, the *Massachusetts* dueled with the French battleship *Jean Bart* at Casablanca. The massive fragment above is from a 16-inch shell that penetrated the *Jean Bart*'s armored deck.

In battle the captain of the *Massachusetts* would command his ship from the heavily armored room shown below.

USS *Lionfish* (SS298)

Classification:	Submarine, Balao class
Sister Ships:	*Batfish* (SS310), *Becuna* (SS319), *Bowfin* (SS287), *Clamagore* (SS343), *Ling* (SS297), *Pampanito* (SS383)
Crew:	6 officers, 60 enlisted men
Length:	311 feet 9 inches
Beam:	27 feet 3 inches
Draft:	15 fcct 3 inches
Displacement:	1,526 tons (2,424 tons when submerged)
Engines:	4 diesel engines and 252 battery cells
Power:	20.25 knots (23 mph) maximum speed when surfaced; approximately 8.75 knots (10 mph) when running on batteries while submerged
Armament:	Twenty-four torpedoes (ten torpedo tubes with fourteen reloads) Antiaircraft guns (an assortment of 5", 40mm, and .50 caliber)

Named for a scorpaenid fish found in the waters off the West Indies and in the tropical Pacific, the USS *Lionfish* was built by the Cramp Shipbuilding Company in Philadelphia, Pennsylvania, and commissioned on November 1, 1944. After completing her shakedown training off the New England coast, the submarine transitted the Panama Canal and arrived in Pearl Harbor on February 25, 1945.

Her first war patrol (March 10–May 15, 1945) took the *Lionfish* to Saipan. After evading two torpedoes fired at her by an enemy submarine, the *Lionfish* attacked a Japanese schooner in the Yellow Sea. In early May she served as part of a lifeguard team assigned to rescue downed airmen off Shanghai.

After refueling at Saipan, the *Lionfish* headed for Midway and then on to Bungo-suido. On July 10, 1945, she attacked and sank an enemy submarine, a hit that was not officially recorded, however, because it could not be confirmed. From mid-July until wartime hostilities ended on August 15, 1945, the *Lionfish* participated in lifeguard duty off the coast of Japan near Honshu. The submarine returned to the West Coast and was decommissioned on January 16, 1946.

Called out of retirement on January 31, 1951, the *Lionfish* served as a training ship in the waters along the East Coast until October 1951. During the summer and fall of 1952, she cruised to Bermuda and Nassau and participated in NATO exercises in the Mediterranean. In June 1953 the submarine returned to Boston, where she was decommissioned on December 15, 1953. The Navy struck her from the official register in 1971 and transferred her to the memorial committee of Fall River, Massachusetts, in 1972.

The USS *Massachusetts* and the USS *Lionfish* are open to the public for tours at Battleship Cove, off Interstate 195 in Fall River, Massachusetts. Also open for tours is a destroyer named for the oldest brother of John F. Kennedy, the USS *Joseph P. Kennedy, Jr.* (DD850), that was launched in 1945 and served in the Korean and Vietnam wars. The park also includes two World War II PT-boats; a World War II landing craft (LCM56); a marine museum; and World War II, Korean War, and Vietnam War memorials.

Crewed by tourists, the *Lionfish* is shown here beside the battleship *Massachusetts*.

USS *Intrepid* (CV11)

Classification:	Aircraft carrier, Essex class (short-hull group)
Sister Ship:	*Yorktown* (CV10)
Crew:	3,348 (officers, enlisted men, and airmen)
Length:	898 feet
Beam:	152 feet at flight deck; 103 feet at hull
Draft:	31 feet
Displacement:	27,100 tons (42,000 tons when fully loaded for combat)
Engines:	8 boilers
Power:	150,000 HP for maximum speed of more than 30 knots (35 mph)
Armament:	Antiaircraft guns (an assortment of 5", 40mm, 20mm) Fifty aircraft Two launching catapults
Wartime Achievements:	Earned five Battle Stars
Nickname:	"Fighting I"

Named for a U.S. ship that was destroyed in a battle with Barbary Coast pirates at Tripoli in 1804, the USS *Intrepid* was built by the Newport News Shipbuilding and Drydock Company in Virginia at a cost of approximately $44 million. Commissioned on August 16, 1943, the carrier completed her shakedown cruise off the East Coast and then steamed through the Panama Canal to join the Pacific Fleet at Pearl Harbor.

In her first wartime action, the *Intrepid* launched her planes to give air cover for the U.S. troops invading the Marshall Islands (January 29, 1944). The *Intrepid*'s planes also participated in the massive air attack against the Japanese-held island of Truk on February 16, 1944. As the carrier was withdrawing after the raid, an enemy torpedo damaged her rudder, forcing her to retreat to Pearl Harbor for temporary repairs and then to California for major work.

Rejoining the Fast Carrier Task Force of the Pacific Fleet in late August 1944, the *Intrepid* launched air attacks on the Palau Islands and Japanese strongholds in the Philippines. In September 1944 the *Intrepid* and the other ships in her task force returned to the Palau Islands and

provided support for the Marines in their invasion of Peleliu. In October 1944 the *Intrepid*'s task force participated in air raids on Formosa that destroyed 600 enemy aircraft and twenty-four ships. The task force also provided support for U.S. landings on Leyte.

In the Battle for Leyte Gulf (October 23–27, 1944), aircraft from the *Intrepid* played a key role in locating the Japanese main fighting force and sinking the superbattleship *Musashi* and other ships. In this battle, which is considered to be the largest naval battle in history, the U.S. forces won a decisive victory, destroying four Japanese aircraft carriers, four battleships, ten cruisers, nine destroyers, and hundreds of aircraft.

On October 29, 1944, several gunners (volunteers from the ship's mess) were killed as they fought off a kamikaze attack on the *Intrepid*. During a mass kamikaze attack on November 25, 1944, two enemy planes crashed into the carrier in less than five minutes, killing six offi-

The *Intrepid* slices through the Pacific one day before launching planes to cover the U.S. invasion of the Marshall Islands in January, 1944.

This burning Japanese Zeke is about to crash into the deck of the carrier *Intrepid*. A piece of the left wing has been blown away by antiaircraft fire.

cers and fifty-nine crewmen, wounding eighty-one others, and sending the *Intrepid* back to the West Coast for repairs.

The carrier rejoined the fleet in February 1945, in time to send her planes to assault Okinawa in preparation for the American invasion of the island. On April 6, 1945, she helped sink the superbattleship *Yamato*, but on April 16, 1945, another kamikaze hit killed eight of her crewmen, injured twenty-two others, and forced the carrier back to Pearl Harbor for repairs. The *Intrepid* returned to service to participate in the attack on Wake Island, August 1, 1945, two weeks before the Japanese surrendered.

The carrier was decommissioned from wartime service in 1947, but between 1951 and 1954, she underwent major modifications that converted her into a modern attack carrier (CVA). Equipped to carry modern aircraft, the *Intrepid* served with the Second Fleet in the Atlantic, the Sixth Fleet in the Mediterranean, and as a prime recovery

Flames roll skyward from the flight deck after a kamikaze Zeke hits the *Intrepid*.

vessel for NASA's Mercury Space Program. On May 24, 1962, the carrier recovered Scott Carpenter and his *Aurora 7* Mercury capsule. In October 1962, she served with other ships in the naval blockade to stop the delivery of Soviet missiles to Cuba.

Between 1963 and 1968, the *Intrepid* underwent several more modifications, converted first into an antisubmarine carrier (CVS), and then modified for special combat tours off the coast of Vietnam. Serving a second time as a prime recovery vessel on March 23, 1965, the carrier picked up Gus Grissom and John Young in their *Gemini 3* space capsule, nicknamed the "Unsinkable Molly Brown." Refitted for antisubmarine duties in 1969, the *Intrepid* served with the Sixth Fleet in the Mediterranean until she was decommissioned and placed on reserve in March 1974.

The *Intrepid* came out of retirement in 1975 to serve as the official U.S. Navy and Marine Corps Bicentennial Exposition Vessel at Philadelphia, where she hosted thousands of visitors throughout 1976. In 1979, New York builder and philanthropist Zachary Fisher helped establish the Intrepid Museum Foundation to bring the *Intrepid* to New York City as both a memorial and educational facility. The Navy struck the carrier from the official register in 1980 and transferred her to the foundation on April 27, 1981. After major restoration was completed, the carrier moved to her specially prepared berth at Pier 86 (West Forty-sixth Street and Twelfth Avenue) in New York City. The *Intrepid* opened to the public as the Intrepid Sea-Air-Space Museum in August 1982.

The *Intrepid* crew fights dozens of fires after a kamikaze attack off Luzon on November 25, 1944.

USS *The Sullivans* (DD537)

Classification:	Destroyer, Fletcher class
Sister Ships:	*Kidd* (DD661), *Cassin Young* (DD793)
Crew:	20 officers, 290 enlisted men
Length:	376 feet 6 inches
Beam:	39 feet
Draft:	24–27 feet
Displacement:	2,050 tons (approximately 3,000 tons when fully loaded for combat)
Engines:	4 boilers, 2 steam-driven turbines
Power:	35 knots (40 mph) maximum speed
Armament:	Five 5" guns Five 40mm twin-mounted antiaircraft guns Seven 20mm single-mounted antiaircraft guns Ten 21" torpedo tubes Six MK6 depth-charge projectors Two MK3 depth-charge tracks
Wartime Achievements:	Earned seven Battle Stars
Nickname:	"Lucky Shamrock"

Named in honor of five brothers who went down together on the torpedoed cruiser *Juneau*, the destroyer *The Sullivans* sails proudly in the Pacific.

When the keel of this destroyer was laid, she was designated the *Putnam,* but President Franklin Roosevelt renamed her the USS *The Sullivans* in memory of five brothers who died aboard the cruiser *Juneau* (CL52), which was sunk by a Japanese submarine while fighting off Guadalcanal on November 13, 1942. Mr. and Mrs. Thomas F. Sullivan, of Waterloo, Iowa, sponsored the ship in honor of their sons Joseph, Francis, Albert, Madison, and George. On the day that *The Sullivans* launched, Mrs. Sullivans carried a "lucky shamrock," a good-luck symbol that was painted on the ship's forward stack.

Commissioned on September 30, 1943, *The Sullivans* served in the Pacific Fleet until the end of World War II. Her crew, which included twenty-three men named Sullivan, participated in battle and rescue operations in the Marshall, Caroline, and Mariana islands and the Philippines. *The Sullivans,* which was not seriously damaged on any of her missions, earned seven battle stars for her outstanding wartime service.

After World War II ended, *The Sullivans* was modernized and assigned to serve in the Korean War and the Cuban Blockade. Decommissioned in 1965, the destroyer is now open to the public for tours. Even though the preserved ship retains most of her 1950s and 1960s modifications, exhibits onboard recall *The Sullivans'* World War II history.

British and American prisoners of war are rescued by a U.S. vessel on September 15, 1944. The prisoners had been aboard a Japanese transport that was torpedoed by a U.S. Navy submarine.

USS *Croaker* (SS246)

Classification:	Submarine, Gato class (modified to SSK246 under the Hunter-Killer conversion program in the 1950s)
Sister Ships:	*Cavalla* (SS244), *Cobia* (SS245), *Cod* (SS224), *Drum* (SS228), *Silversides* (SS236)
Crew:	7 officers, 65 enlisted men
Length:	306 feet 6 inches
Beam:	27 feet 2 inches
Draft:	Approximately 16 feet
Displacement:	Approximately 1,500 tons (more than 2,000 tons when submerged)
Engines:	4 diesel engines and 250 battery cells
Power:	Approximately 6,500 HP from diesel engines for 20 knots (23 mph) maximum speed when surfaced; approximately 9 knots (6 mph) maximum speed when running on batteries while submerged
Armament:	Twenty-four torpedoes (ten torpedo tubes with fourteen reloads) One 5" gun One 40mm antiaircraft gun One 20mm antiaircraft gun
Wartime Achievements:	Earned three Battle Stars and the Navy Unit commendation, completed six war patrols, sank 40,000 tons of enemy shipping

Named for a family of fish (Sciaenidae) that makes croaking noises, the USS *Croaker* was built by the Electric Boat Company in Groton, Connecticut, at a cost of approximately $6.3 million. Commissioned on April 21, 1944, the submarine left the East Coast and joined the Pacific Fleet.

On August 7, 1944, she sank the Japanese cruiser *Nagara*. By the end of the war, she had sunk eleven enemy vessels for an official total of 40,000 tons. The *Croaker* completed six war patrols, earning three battle stars for her outstanding service.

In 1953 the submarine was modernized with a streamlined sail, snorkel, and updated radar system. Between December 1953 and 1968 the *Croaker* completed routine cruises in the Atlantic, Caribbean, and Mediterranean.

The submarine served as a training ship for the Naval Reserve from 1968 until the Navy decommissioned her on December 20, 1971. The Submarine Memorial Association of Groton, Connecticut, obtained possession of the ship on June 27, 1976. The *Croaker* was transferred to the Buffalo and Erie County Naval and Servicemen's Park in November 1988 and is now open to the public for tours.

USS *Little Rock* (CL92)

Classification:	Light cruiser, Cleveland class (modified to Talos guided missile cruiser CLG4 between 1957 and 1960)
Crew:	150 officers, 1100 enlisted men, 150 Marines
Length:	610 feet
Beam:	66 feet
Draft:	20 feet
Displacement:	10,000 tons (12, 000 tons when fully loaded for combat)
Engines:	8 boilers
Power:	100,000 HP maximum, 33 knots (38 mph) maximum speed
Armament:	Twelve 6" guns
	Twelve 5" guns in twin mounts
	Twenty-four 40mm antiaircraft guns
	Nineteen 20mm antiaircraft guns
	Three aircraft
	Two launching catapults

Named for the city of Little Rock, Arkansas, this light cruiser was built by the Cramp Shipbuilding Company in Philadelphia, Pennsylvania, at a cost of approximately $31 million. The USS *Little Rock* was commissioned in June 1945, just a few months before the end of World War II. The cruiser continued on active duty until she was decommissioned in 1949.

In late January 1957, the *Little Rock* returned to Philadelphia for conversion to a guided-missile cruiser. With the capability of firing powerful 30-foot-long Talos missiles, the *Little Rock* completed four missions in the Mediterranean and two in the North Atlantic and served as the flagship for both the Second and Sixth fleets. Relieved of her flagship duties in August 1970, the *Little Rock* underwent a major overhaul at the naval yard in Boston and then returned to the Mediterranean. The Navy decommissioned the cruiser on November 22, 1976, and struck her from the official register. The preserved ship is now open to the public at the Naval and Servicemen's Park in Buffalo. The *Little Rock* retains her postwar modifications, with only her bow, a single 6-inch turret, and a single 5-inch turret remaining from her World War II configuration.

USS *The Sullivans*, USS *Croaker*, and USS *Little Rock* are berthed at the Buffalo and Erie County Naval and Servicemen's Park, at the foot of Pearl Street (off Interstate 190) and the Buffalo River in Buffalo. The park also includes a museum and exhibits of vintage aircraft, a 1970s PT-boat, and other military equipment.

HACKENSACK, NEW JERSEY

USS *Ling* (SS297)

Classification:	Submarine, Balao class
Sister Ships:	*Batfish* (SS310), *Becuna* (SS319), *Lionfish* (SS298), *Clamagore* (SS343), *Bowfin* (SS287), *Pampanito* (SS383)
Crew:	95 officers and enlisted men
Length:	312 feet
Beam:	27 feet
Draft:	Approximately 16 feet
Displacement:	1,526 tons (2,424 tons when submerged)
Engines:	4 diesel engines and 252 battery cells
Power:	20 knots (23 mph) maximum speed when surfaced; approximately 10 knots (12 mph) when running on batteries while submerged
Armament:	Twenty-four torpedoes (ten torpedo tubes with fourteen reloads) Antiaircraft guns (an assortment of 5", 3", 40mm, and 20mm)

Torpedo tubes aboard the *Ling*

One of the last fleet-type submarines authorized for service during World War II, the USS *Ling* was built by the Cramp Shipbuilding Company in Philadelphia and outfitted at the Navy Yard in Boston. Commissioned on June 8, 1945, the *Ling* completed one patrol with the Atlantic Fleet before the war ended.

The Navy decommissioned the submarine on October 15, 1946, and placed her in the New London Group of the Atlantic Reserve Fleet. In 1960 the Navy recalled the *Ling* to active service as a training vessel for Naval Reserve Submarine Divisions 2-23 and 3-55 at the Brooklyn Navy Yard.

On December 1, 1971, the Navy again decommissioned the submarine and struck her from the official register. Members of the Submarine Memorial Association in Hackensack, New Jersey, asked that the *Ling* be donated for use as a memorial and spearheaded a drive to raise the funds necessary to prepare a permanent site for the ship. The submarine was towed to its berth on the Hackensack River in January 1973. Restored to her World War II appearance, the *Ling* was designated the official state naval museum on October 17, 1988. The ship is open to the public at Borg Park, at the intersection of Court and River streets in Hackensack.

The *Ling* at its memorial berth in Hackensack, New Jersey

The typical U.S. Navy World War II submarine periscope played a vital role in sinking enemy tonnage.

CHAPTER TWO

SILENT AND DEEP

Almost half a century after stalking Japanese convoys in the Pacific with Chester Nimitz, Jr., Bill Mack is still a submariner. He guides visitors through the USS *Becuna* in Philadelphia. Mack put in most of his World War II service aboard the submarine *Haddo*, which once sank seven Japanese ships in a single run out of Fremantle, Australia.

"First you had to get past their destroyer escorts. Usually you'd sneak in on the surface, just as close in as you could to their transports. With the right kind of weather, you could get in as close as 700 yards. You'd fire your torpedoes—one, two, three, four—maybe one or two seconds apart. Then, whether you hit anything or not, you had to pull the plug and get out of there because you knew they'd be coming after you." That was how Bill Mack described the proper technique for attacking a Japanese convoy at night.

Nowadays Mack leads wide-eyed children and curious adults on tours of the memorialized submarine *Becuna* in Philadelphia. He points to this lever, that switch, these gauges and explains what they are for and how they work. He cracks jokes. But during World War II, his job was guiding submarines, not visitors. An experienced helmsman, he maneuvered the *Haddo* (SS255) in for kills on Japanese shipping.

During part of Mack's time in the Pacific, his commanding officer was Chester Nimitz, Jr., son of the famous admiral. "Nimitz was the most aggressive skipper we ever had," said Mack. "On a single run out of Fremantle [in Australia] we sank seven ships. We were doing so well, Nimitz asked the crew if we wanted to stay out and keep on with the hunt. Even though we'd already been out fifty-two days, every last man told the skipper to keep going."

With this vote of confidence from his men, Nimitz took the *Haddo* briefly into the Australian port of Darwin for fuel and provisions. "Mostly we needed more torpedoes," said Mack.

Soon, Nimitz and the *Haddo* crew were putting their fresh supply of torpedoes to use. They sank at least one additional ship and damaged others. "We would run out in front of their convoys, submerge, and wait for the enemy ships to pass over us. Then we would surface and hit them."

Often the Japanese struck back furiously. "They always did. They would work us over for hours. The depth charges made a hellish noise and shook everything up—like there was a war going on or something. The concussions would throw people around, knock pots and pans out of the galley, and break lightbulbs. You'd get leaks. With all that going on, you could literally crap in your pants. It was nothing to be ashamed of to crap your pants."

Mack said a sailor from another submarine once told him of a depth charging so severe that it smashed fourteen bottles of whiskey the crew had secreted on board and hidden in the engine room. After the attack, the captain found one of his men in tears. The skipper put an arm around the man and said "It's okay, son, it's all over now."

Life aboard a World War II submarine was cramped, to say the least. This is the crew's mess on the *Ling*.

"I don't care about the depth charges," the sailor replied, never taking his eyes off the shattered bottles. "Look what they did to our booze!"

Submarine crews were very young. A captain might be little more than thirty, but his men were a lot younger. "The captain was like a father who had eighty-eight or eighty-nine kids. You had tough skippers and others who were not so tough, but there was never much of a problem with discipline on submarines because everybody depended on everybody else."

Some skippers, like Nimitz, had a hardy sense of humor. Mack remembers a practical joke that Nimitz had sprung on him. "I hated the brass smell the helm left on my hands, so I decided to wrap it [with cord]. It took a long time, and guys kept coming by to ask me what I was doing. Finally, I got tired of hearing the same question over and over."

Mack started barking at his fellow crewmen, telling them to mind their own business. Noticing Mack's irritation, Nimitz walked quietly up behind the helmsman and, in a disguised voice, asked, "What's that you're doing, sailor?"

Mack exploded. "Can't you see what I'm doing, you simpleminded son of a bitch?"

"What was that you said!" asked Nimitz, reverting to his normal voice. "I'm a simpleminded what?"

Recognizing the captain, Mack drew in a deep breath. "I said I'm wrapping the wheel, sir!"

Submarine crews used humor, hard work, and their youthful high spirits to get them through the tension of combat and the long weeks of confinement during extended patrols, often lasting sixty days or more.

American submarines carried food and fuel for ninety days. Fresh water, however, was almost always in short supply. "You could go five weeks without a shower," said Mack. "And when you did get a shower, it lasted about fifteen seconds."

A hot shower was among the rewards waiting for the crew after a lengthy combat run. The men were treated to fresh milk, fruit, ice cream, and other such delicacies they had not tasted for months. "They also threw us a beer bust, and usually this would last until no one was left standing."

Crewmen were given a brief rest ashore while the damage done to their submarine by enemy and ocean was hurriedly repaired. Then it was back to sea again for another long, lonely patrol.

At sea, vigilance had to be continuous. "Once outside the harbor, a submarine has no friends," said Mack. "You could just as easily be sunk by our own ships or planes as by those of the enemy." In fact, the *Haddo* was, on one occasion, strafed and damaged by an American Corsair fighter.

But the *Haddo* and Mack both made it through the war. The *Haddo* was eventually scrapped. Mack went back to Philadelphia, his hometown. The department store where he had worked before the war promised to give him back his job, but only at 1941 wages. The rapid postwar inflation made the offer worthless, and Mack turned it down. "In the end, all I got was my name on a plaque by the elevator."

Control room on the *Ling*

Job or no job, Mack considers himself very fortunate to have made it home at all. Many submarine crewmen did not. A bronze marker beside the *Becuna*'s Delaware River berth lists the fifty-two American submarines that put to sea during World War II and never returned. Ironically, two of these, the *Durado* and *Seawolf,* were lost to the mistaken fire of friendly forces. One American sub was even sunk by its own errant torpedo. Enemy bombs and torpedoes probably destroyed most of the others. During the course of the war, at least 374 officers and 3,131 crewmen went down with their submarines. Veterans consider these men and their subs to be "still on patrol."

The submarine *Becuna* offers a stark contrast to the nineteenth-century cruiser *Olympia*, which served as Commodore Dewey's flagship during the Spanish-American War. During the four decades that separated the service eras of the two vessels, naval warfare changed completely.

USS *Becuna* (SS319)

Classification:	Submarine, Balao class (modified into a Guppy IA in 1951)
Sister Ships:	*Batfish* (SS310), *Bowfin* (SS287), *Clamagore* (SS343), *Ling* (SS297), *Lionfish* (SS298), *Pampanito* (SS383)
Crew:	8 officers, 72 enlisted men
Length:	308 feet
Beam:	27 feet
Draft:	Approximately 16 feet
Displacement:	1,526 tons (approximately 2,400 when submerged)
Engines:	4 diesel engines and 252 battery cells
Power:	20 knots (23 mph) maximum speed when surfaced; approximately 10 knots (12 mph) when running on batteries while submerged
Armament:	Twenty-four torpedoes (ten torpedo tubes with fourteen reloads) Antiaircraft guns (an assortment of 5", 3", 40mm, and 20mm)
Wartime Achievements:	Earned four Battle Stars and a Presidential Unit Citation, destroyed thousands of tons of Japanese naval and merchant ships

Built by the Electric Boat Company at Groton, Connecticut, the USS *Becuna* was commissioned on May 27, 1944, as the submarine flagship of the Southwest Pacific Fleet under General Douglas MacArthur. From August 23, 1944, to July 27, 1945, the *Becuna* patrolled the waters off the Philippines, as well as the South China and Java seas. During her five war missions, she sank thousands of tons of enemy fighting and merchant ships.

The *Becuna* continued to serve the Navy after the end of World War II. In 1949 she patrolled the Caribbean as part of the Atlantic Fleet and then cruised with the Sixth Fleet in the Mediterranean and off the coast of Scotland.

The addition of a snorkel air system, large electric battery, and updated radar, fire control, and torpedo equipment (with nuclear warheads) in 1951 converted the *Becuna* from a Fleet-type submarine to the streamlined, faster configuration of a Guppy IA. After serving on missions in both the Atlantic and Mediterranean during the Korean and Vietnam wars, the *Becuna* returned to her home port in Connecticut and served as a training ship.

The *Becuna* was decommissioned in 1969 and is now open to the public at Penn's Landing, in Philadelphia. Also berthed at the site are the restored USS *Olympia* (the cruiser that served as Commodore George Dewey's flagship during the Spanish-American War), the *Gazela Primero* (an 1883 Portuguese square-rigger), the lightship *Barnegat*, and the *Moshulu* (a 1904 four-masted, all-steel sailing ship). The ships include naval exhibits.

BALTIMORE, MARYLAND

USS *Torsk* (SS423)

Classification:	Submarine, Tench class
Crew:	8 officers, 82 enlisted men
Length:	311 feet 2 inches
Beam:	27 feet 2 inches
Draft:	Approximately 17 feet
Displacement:	1,800 tons (2,500 tons when submerged)
Engines:	4 diesel engines and 252 battery cells
Power:	20.25 knots (23 mph) maximum speed when surfaced; 8.75 knots (10 mph) maximum speed when running on batteries while submerged
Armament:	Twenty-four torpedoes (ten torpedo tubes with fourteen reloads) Antiaircraft guns (an assortment of 5", 3", 40mm, and 20mm)
Wartime Achievements:	Earned two Battle Stars, completed two war patrols, credited with firing the last torpedo and sinking the last enemy ship during the war

The *Torsk* shows its teeth at the Baltimore Maritime Museum in the Inner Harbor.

Named for a gadoid (codlike) fish found in the North Atlantic, the USS *Torsk* was built at the Portsmouth Naval Shipyard, in Portsmouth, New Hampshire, and commissioned on December 16, 1944. After completing her shakedown training along the East Coast, the submarine transitted the Panama Canal and joined the Pacific Fleet at Pearl Harbor on March 23, 1945.

Her first war patrol (April 5–June 16, 1945) took the *Torsk* to the waters off the Japanese coast on lifeguard duty to rescue B-29 airmen downed in air raids. During her second patrol (July 17–August 15, 1945), the *Torsk* patrolled the Sea of Japan, where she rescued seven Japanese sailors and sank three enemy ships totaling 2,473 tons. The *Torsk*'s torpedo that sank the third ship was the last torpedo fired during the war, and the target was the last enemy vessel sunk during the war.

Much bigger than any of the fish in the adjacent National Aquarium in Baltimore, the *Torsk* looms quite large in this view. It's a different story, however, in the claustrophobic quarters below deck.

A life jacket snatched from this jumble might have saved a sailor from certain death in World War II.

In the period following the cease-fire order that ended wartime aggressions, the *Torsk* briefly patrolled off the coast of Japan and then returned to the East Coast. From 1945 to 1955 she served with the Submarine School at New London, Connecticut, where she made several training dives a day for a record total of 11,884 dives. Known as the "divingest" submarine in the Navy, the *Torsk* was converted to a Guppy configuration with a snorkel in November 1951.

The *Torsk* participated in NATO exercises in 1957 and the opening of the St. Lawrence Seaway in 1959. During the Lebanon Crisis in 1960, she worked with the Sixth Fleet in the Mediterranean, and during the Missile Crisis of 1962 she was assigned to help blockade Cuba.

The Navy decommissioned the *Torsk* on December 15, 1971, and placed her in the reserve fleet. The state of Maryland obtained possession of the submarine in September 1972 and opened her to the public at the Baltimore Maritime Museum in the city's Inner Harbor.

USCGC *Taney* (WHEC37)

Classification:	Coast Guard cutter
Sister Ship:	*Ingham* (WHEC35)
Crew:	12 officers, 117 enlisted men
Length:	327 feet
Beam:	41 feet
Draft:	12 feet 6 inches
Displacement:	2,700 tons
Engines:	2 boilers
Power:	6,200 HP for 20 knots (23 mph) maximum speed
Armament:	One 5" gun Two .50-caliber machine guns
Wartime Achievements:	Credited with fighting off five enemy planes during the Japanese attack on Pearl Harbor, December 7, 1941; completed numerous wartime convoy missions in both the Atlantic and the Pacific

Named in honor of Roger B. Taney, who served as U.S. Secretary of the Treasury and Chief Justice of the Supreme Court, the USCGC *Taney* was built at the naval shipyard at Philadelphia and commissioned on Octo-

ber 24, 1936. Operating out of her home port of Honolulu, the cutter was anchored in Pearl Harbor when the Japanese attacked early in the morning of December 7, 1941. The *Taney* is credited with fighting off five enemy planes that were headed toward the Honolulu Power Plant.

The cutter served on convoy duty in both the Atlantic and the Pacific during the war. She successfully completed numerous missions through the German U-boat–infested waters of the North Atlantic.

When the war ended, the *Taney* resumed her peacetime assignments, which included manning ocean stations in the Pacific. During the Korean War (1950–1953), she provided communication and meteorological services for U.S. forces, and during the Vietnam War, she participated in Operation Market Time (April 1969–February 1970) in the waters off the Philippines and Vietnam.

Working out of home ports on the East Coast in the 1970s, the *Taney* resumed her normal law enforcement, search and rescue, and training duties. After fifty years of service, the cutter was decommissioned on December 7, 1986. The preserved ship is at the Baltimore Maritime Museum at the city's Inner Harbor.

The Coast Guard cutter *Taney*, shown above in Baltimore, fought back as fiercely as any Navy ship during the Japanese attack on Pearl Harbor.

SS *John W. Brown* (Liberty Ship)

Classification:	Liberty Ship
Sister Ship:	*Jeremiah O'Brien*
Crew:	81 men
Length:	441 feet 6 inches
Beam:	56 feet 11 inches
Draft:	27 feet 9 inches
Displacement:	14,257 tons
Engines:	3-cylinder triple expansion reciprocating steam engine
Power:	2,500 HP for maximum speed of 11 knots (13 mph)

This poster displayed on the *John W. Brown* speaks for itself. Liberty Ships were a favorite prey of German U-boats.

One of the more than 2,700 Liberty Ships designed to carry cargo—food, fuel, tanks, trucks, jeeps, airplane parts, bombs, mules, horses, ammunition, and later, troops, prisoners of war, and war brides—the SS *John W. Brown* was built at the Bethlehem-Fairfield shipyard in Baltimore. Named in honor of John W. Brown, who was prominent in the American Labor movement at the turn of the century, the ship was launched on Labor Day, September 7, 1942. Carrying a full load of tanks and ammunition, she left on September 28, 1942, for the Persian Gulf, taking a roundabout route (through the Panama Canal, down the west coast of South America, across the South Atlantic, and around Cape Horn) to avoid German U-boats.

After almost nine months of carrying cargo to ports around the world, the *Brown* was converted to a troopship. From June 1943 until the end of the war, the Liberty Ship made eight wartime voyages in the Mediterranean, carrying troops and cargo between North Africa, Sicily, Italy, and France. The *Brown* also supported invasions at Anzio and Salerno in Italy and at beaches along the southern coast of France.

When the war ended, the Liberty Ship contributed to the rebuilding of Europe by continuing to carry needed supplies to wartorn areas. In December 1946 the *Brown* was transferred to the city of New York, where she served as a floating nautical high school providing hands-on training in seamanship and engineering.

Project Liberty Ship was organized in 1978 to preserve the *Brown*, one of only a few Liberty Ships remaining in existence. On August 13, 1988, the *Brown* was towed to Baltimore, where she is anchored at Pier One on Clinton Street.

The odd-looking material below the sign and decorations is "plastic armor." This asphaltlike substance replaced metal armoring on some Liberty Ships because steel was in short supply.

A 5-inch gun rests in silence on the *John W. Brown*. It is said the *Brown* fought a daylong duel with German artillery in the hills above Anzio, Italy.

CHAPTER THREE

BIG SHOW ON THE SHOWBOAT

Tokyo Rose delivered the warning in her silkiest voice: "I've got some very bad news for you men aboard the mysterious Battleship *X*," she would say. Then she would give them the bad news. Usually it was some sort of veiled threat: mines and torpedoes lurking just beneath the waves, fiery death about to streak down out of the clouds. Would the men of the Battleship *X* ever see their homes again? She hoped so.

"A lot of what Rose said was meant to keep us guessing," said Paul Wieser, who served five years aboard the enormous warship known to the U.S. Navy as the *North Carolina* or BB-55 and to its crew as the "Showboat." Wieser firmly believes the *North Carolina* had another name as well. He doesn't have to guess about that. He is absolutely convinced the *North Carolina* was Rose's mysterious Battleship *X*.

It may be that sailors on every battleship in the Pacific imagined they were standing on the deck of the mysterious *X* and that Rose's cooing taunts were aimed directly at them. The crew of the USS *South Dakota* staked the strongest claim to the title—unfairly, in Wieser's opinion—when their ship returned to the United States for repairs. The war was still raging, and newspapers were hungry for headlines about the Pacific front. The men of the *South Dakota* gave them one. They told reporters the *South Dakota* was Tokyo Rose's Battleship *X*. But Wieser knows Rose was speaking to the *North Carolina* when she said the *X* had been sunk. "She said it two or three times, but that was all

This is how the battleship *North Carolina* appeared in 1961, not long after it was towed to its permanent berth in Wilmington.

lies, of course. The Japanese tried to sink us, all right, but they could not do it."

The *North Carolina* was damaged by enemy fire only a few times during the war and only once seriously, by a torpedo. Japanese bombers and torpedo planes had little chance against the Showboat. The big ship had dozens of 20mm and 40mm guns capable of firing a withering barrage of antiaircraft fire. Their aim assisted by radar, the *North Carolina*'s 5-inch guns, paired in ten separate turrets, would blow an enemy plane to fragments long before it got a chance to drop a bomb on the ship's heavily armored deck. Wieser's battle station was in one of the 5-inch turrets on the ship's starboard side. He says he "can't count" the times he sweated inside that turret as its guns pounded away at bombers and kamikazes.

There was little the gunners could do, however, to stop a torpedo, especially one that seemed to appear from nowhere. On September 15, 1942, during an action off Guadalcanal, the U.S. carrier *Wasp* had just turned into the wind and was about to launch her planes. As the *Wasp* turned, she temporarily lost her "screen" of destroyers, and unknowingly, lined up in the sights of the *I-19*, a submerged Japanese submarine. Immediately, Commander Takaichi Kinashi, captain of the *I-19*, sent a fanlike spread of six torpedoes racing toward the doomed *Wasp*. Three of the torpedoes found their mark, fatally wounding the carrier, while three others missed, or so Kinahi believed.

The large "long lance" torpedoes—U.S. sailors sometimes called them "Long Toms"—used by Japanese submarines had a range of more than twelve miles. When the *I-19* attacked the *Wasp*, the *North Carolina* and the destroyer *O'Brien* were several miles away, almost out of sight. As crewmen on the deck of the *North Carolina* heard the distant thunder of the explosions as the *Wasp* was hit, they may have wondered if torpedoes were also cutting through the water toward them. They did not have long to wait for the answer. Minutes later, a tremendous explosion blew off the bow of the *O'Brien*. Moments after that, another explosion tore a gaping 32-foot hole in the side of the *North Carolina*. It is now believed, though it has never been proven, that the battleship and destroyer were hit by *I-19* torpedoes that had missed the *Wasp*.

The *North Carolina,* which had five casualties in the attack, returned to Pearl Harbor for repairs. The *O'Brien* sank while returning to the United States. Eventually, the *I-19* itself was sunk by American depth charges.

Commander Kinashi won considerable acclaim for sinking the *Wasp*. Later in the war, he gave up command of the *I-19* and was sent on a special mission to La Rochelle, in France, to pick up secret blueprints for a new fighter plane designed by Japan's German allies. Kinashi successfully navigated a small submarine halfway around the world to France. He had almost made it back to Japan when three American submarines trapped and sank his vessel off Luzon in the Philippines.

In 1986, Wieser met two Japanese veterans who had been aboard the *I-19* on the day the *Wasp,* the *North Carolina,* and the *O'Brien* were torpedoed. The Japanese had come to Wilmington to visit the memorialized battleship *North Carolina.*

"We smiled and shook hands," said Wieser. Then he gave them a tour of the ship their armed forces had damaged but had never managed to sink—the mysterious Battleship *X.*

Kingfisher float plane at the stern of the *North Carolina*

WILMINGTON, NORTH CAROLINA

USS *North Carolina* (BB55)

Classification:	Battleship, North Carolina class
Sister Ship:	USS *Washington* (BB56)
Crew:	144 officers, 2,195 enlisted men (including about 100 Marines)
Length:	728 feet $8^5/_8$ inches
Beam:	108 feet $3^7/_8$ inches
Displacement:	36,600 tons (44,800 tons when fully loaded for combat)
Engines:	4 engine rooms, each with 2 boilers and 1 turbine
Power:	121,000 HP maximum, 28 knots (32 mph) maximum speed
Armament:	Nine 16" guns in three triple turrets (21 miles, maximum range) Twenty 5" guns in ten twin mounts Sixty 40mm antiaircraft machine guns in fifteen quadruple mounts (as of June 1945) Thirty-six 20mm single antiaircraft machine guns (as of June 1945) Three OS2U (Vought Kingfisher) aircraft Two launching catapults
Wartime Achievements:	Earned fifteen Battle Stars, shot down twenty-four enemy planes, participated in nine bombardments of Japanese strongholds, sank a Japanese troopship.
Nickname:	"The Showboat"

The third ship to bear the name USS *North Carolina* was built at the New York Navy Yard in Brooklyn, New York, at a cost of almost $77 million. Commissioned on April 9, 1941, the *North Carolina* was the first of ten fast, modern American battleships to be built during World War II. During her extensive shakedown period, the *North Carolina* repeatedly returned to the Brooklyn Navy Yard for consultations, adjustments, and modifications. New Yorkers who noticed the frequent presence of the majestic ship in the harbor started calling her "The Showboat," after the riverboat in a popular Broadway musical. On one occasion the *North Carolina* steamed into the harbor and anchored next to the USS *Washington,* whose crew greeted their sister ship's crew with a chorus of "Here Comes the Showboat." The *North Carolina*'s crew proudly adopted the nickname, which stuck through the wartime years to the present day.

After completing her shakedown, the battleship left New York for Hawaii, arriving in Pearl Harbor on July 11, 1942. The *North Carolina* spent her entire wartime career in the Pacific, where she participated in every major campaign and earned a total of fifteen battle stars for her outstanding service in the landings on Guadalcanal and Tulagi, the cap-

The *North Carolina* was towed toward its display berth in Wilmington only after state citizens, including school children who contributed coins, helped save the battleship from being scrapped.

ture and defense of Guadalcanal, the Battle of the Eastern Solomons, the New Georgia Group Operations (New Guinea, Rendova, Vangunu invasion), the Gilbert Islands Operation (Tarawa and Makin), the Bismarck Archipelago Operations (Kavieng strike), the Marshall Islands Operation (invasion of Kwajalein and Majuro Atolls), Task Force Strikes (Truk, the Marianas, Palau, Yap, Ulithi, Woleai, Satawan, and Ponape), the Western New Guinea Operations (Hollandia), the Marianas Operations (invasion of Saipan and the Battle of the Philippine Sea), the Leyte Operation (attacks on Luzon, Formosa, China Coast, and Nansei Shoto), the Iwo Jima Operation (invasion of Iwo Jima and Fifth and Third Fleet raids on Honshu and Nansei Shoto), the Okinawa Invasion, and the Third Fleet Operations against Japan.

On her first wartime assignment (August 7–9, 1942), the *North Carolina* screened the carriers *Enterprise*, *Saratoga*, and *Wasp* from enemy air and surface attack while aircraft from those ships provided cover for the 19,000 Marines landing on Guadalcanal and Tulagi. The *North Carolina* received her "baptism by fire" in the Battle of the Eastern Solomons when enemy dive-bombers and torpedo planes swarmed down on the *Enterprise* and the battleship. Losing only one crew member to enemy fire, the *North Carolina* shot down seven Japanese planes, assisted in downing at least seven more, and frustrated the attacks of still others. The furious barrage from her massive battery of antiaircraft guns caused the *Enterprise* to signal anxiously asking if the battleship was afire. The *North Carolina* played an important part in saving the *Enterprise* during that battle, establishing the supportive wartime role battleships would assume in protecting carriers.

This is one of the "screws" that helped drive the 36,600-ton *North Carolina* through the ocean at speeds up to 28 knots.

Following the battle, the *North Carolina* remained off Guadalcanal with the aircraft carriers *Saratoga*, *Wasp*, and *Hornet* to cover cargo ships supplying the Marines onshore. On September 15, 1942, Japanese submarines attacked the task force and hit the *North Carolina* with a torpedo, killing five of her crew and forcing her to return to Pearl Harbor for repairs.

On December 9, 1942, the *North Carolina* returned to the waters off Guadalcanal, where she screened the *Enterprise* and *Saratoga* and covered troop and supply movements for the most of the next year. From November 19 through December 8, 1943, the *North Carolina* worked with the *Alabama,* the *Massachusetts,* the *Enterprise,* and other ships in Operation Galvanic, the invasion of the Gilbert Islands. She helped bombard Japanese strongholds at Nauru, Roi, and Namur, and then joined Task Force 58 (which included twelve carriers, eight battleships, six cruisers, and thirty-four destroyers) in attacking Truk, Guam, Saipan, Tinian, Palau, Yap, Ulithi, Woleai, Hollandia, and New Guinea. While bombarding Kwajalein Atoll on January 29, 1944, she sank an enemy troopship. During a strike on Truk on April 30, 1944, the *North Carolina*'s Kingfisher float planes were used to rescue downed U.S. airmen.

After a hurried retreat to Pearl Harbor for repairs, the *North Carolina* rejoined Task Force 58 in June 1944 and helped cover the U.S. invasion of the Mariana Islands. During the "Marianas Turkey Shoot," the opening air confrontation of the Battle of the Philippine Sea (June 19–21, 1944), the *North Carolina* formed a battle line with the *Washington, South Dakota, Indiana, Alabama, Iowa, New Jersey,* four heavy cruisers, and fourteen destroyers. After the decisive U.S. victory, the *North Carolina* steamed to Puget Sound Navy Yard in Bremerton, Washington, for an extensive overhaul.

The *North Carolina* returned to the Western Pacific in November 1944 and endured her first kamikaze attack while guarding the aircraft carriers *Essex, Hancock, Intrepid, Cabot,* and other ships in Task Force 38 assigned to operations in the Philippines. On December 18, 1944, a powerful typhoon hit the task force, capsizing three of the destroyers. The surviving ships steamed to Formosa and the Indochina and China coasts, where they participated in strikes that prepared the way for the assault of Iwo Jima (February 19–22, 1945).

In the assault on Okinawa in April 1945, the *North Carolina* both bombarded the Japanese home islands and provided a screen for aircraft carriers. On April 6, 1945, she downed three kamikazes but, in the midst of antiaircraft fire, took a hit from a friendly ship that killed three men and wounded forty-four others.

The *North Carolina* retired to Pearl Harbor for repairs and then rejoined the Third Fleet to help bombard and support air strikes on Japan (July 10–August 15, 1945). The battleship continued to patrol off the coast for about two weeks before anchoring in Tokyo Bay on September 5, 1945, three days after the Japanese signed the surrender papers onboard the battleship *Missouri.*

On September 6, 1945, the *North Carolina* left for home, stopping in Okinawa to take on passengers. She received a hero's welcome when she arrived in Boston on October 17, 1945. The U.S. Navy decommissioned the battleship on June 27, 1947, and she spent the next fourteen years in the mothball fleet at Bayonne, New Jersey. When the Navy decided to scrap the *North Carolina* in 1960, the citizens of that state launched a "Save Our Ship" campaign and raised $330,000 to acquire the battleship and prepare a berth. In September 1961 the *North Carolina* was towed from New Jersey to the Cape Fear River, where she is permanently moored across from downtown Wilmington. The *North Carolina* was dedicated and opened to the public on April 29, 1962.

The USS *North Carolina* is open daily at Battleship Memorial located about three miles from Wilmington, North Carolina, at the intersection of U.S. routes 17, 74, 76, and 421. Visitors are invited to view a ten-minute orientation film and take a self-guided tour through the ship. "The Immortal Showboat," a sound-and-light show with special effects that tells the story of the *North Carolina,* is presented each evening from the first Friday in June through Labor Day.

INTERLUDE

NAVY CHOW

While young men joined the Navy to defend their country and to "see the world," they also expected to be well fed. The Navy has a reputation for serving up the best chow offered by any of the U.S. armed services, and World War II sailors ate at least as well as those today.

Posted on the wall of the USS *Yorktown* galley is the menu for March 20, 1944. On that day, the men of the carrier *Yorktown* woke up to a breakfast of fruit, cooked cereal, baked meat hash, catsup, boiled eggs, German coffee cake (the wartime aversion to all things German apparently did not extend to pastries), bread, butter, and coffee. For dinner the crew was treated to fried hamburger steak, cottage fried potatoes, fried onions, stewed tomatoes, caramel cake, bread, butter, and coffee. For the entire week beginning March 20, *Yorktown* Supply Officer W. E. Moring reported food costs (not including preparation) of $9,885.05 for feeding nearly 3,000 sailors, an expense of approximately 61 cents per person each day.

Cooking for 3,000 was a big job. The cooks and bakers on the *Yorktown* and other large ships thought in terms of enormous quantities. Consider the following recipe for chocolate chip cookies:

112 lbs. of chocolate chips

165 lbs. flour

500 eggs

100 lbs. granulated sugar

12 lbs. salt

3 cups vanilla extract

$1\frac{1}{2}$ lbs. baking soda

Makes about 10,000 cookies

A baking-powder biscuit recipe posted in the galley of the battleship *North Carolina* called for:

16 lbs. sugar

5 lbs. salt

48 lbs. shortening

200 lbs. flour

22 lbs. baking powder

Most seamen were served cafeteria-style on metal trays that had to be passed through the scullery window after the meal. On a ship the size of the *Yorktown*, 3,000 trays, 3,000 cups, and up to 11,000 utensils were run through the ship's scullery after each meal. Operated by "non-rated personnel," the *Yorktown* scullery washed more than 50,000 items each day.

Officers, of course, were not expected to eat off trays. They took their meals in the ship's ward room, where they enjoyed amenities such as plates, tablecloths, and napkins, and where attentive waiters kept their coffee cups full. Captains and admirals often had personal chefs and ate at private tables, located in or near their quarters.

In combat, meals took on a more democratic aspect. When at battlestations, the entire crew, officers included, were served sack lunches consisting of two sandwiches and a piece of fruit.

CHAPTER FOUR

DAVID AND GOLIATH

When veterans who served on the destroyer *Laffey* hold their annual reunion, the war stories fly. To the uninitiated, however, these tales of danger and daring may seem a bit confusing. The outsider who listens closely soon suspects that all of these men could not have served on the same ship, and that is true. They did not. Just as there have been two *Yorktown*s, there have also been two *Laffey*s. The men of both *Laffey*s sometimes hold their meetings together. After all, their destroyers shared more than a name. Both were battered and bloodied. The first was sunk in 1942 during a night of wild and desperate violence off Guadalcanal. The second was pounded and almost destroyed by kamikaze bombers.

Doc Brown served on the second *Laffey* (DD724). "It was April 16, 1945," said Brown. "The radar had picked up planes about 25 miles out, and we were at battle stations; mine was the after torpedo tubes. We didn't have to wait long. The 20mm [antiaircraft] started up, and then we saw them coming. The first plane in hit us with a bomb and jammed our rudder. After that, all we could do was paddle around in a circle like a duck. The Japanese used us for target practice. In all, we took hits from four bombs and six suicide planes." (The U.S. Navy said the *Laffey* was hit by three bombs and five planes.)

When the attack ended, the *Laffey* was still afloat, but thirty-one members of the crew lay dead, and another seventy-one were wounded. Brown, who was eighteen at the time, was among the seriously wound-

The sun has not set for the last time on "unsinkable" ships such as the *Yorktown*. Once they served as fighting ships; now they serve as inspiration.

Shot to pieces by antiaircraft fire, a Japanese Jill torpedo bomber careens toward the ocean.

ed. Some of the damage done to the ship that day can still be seen by the visitors who pour into Patriots Point Naval and Maritime Museum, near Charleston, South Carolina. There the *Laffey* is preserved and open to the public along with the carrier *Yorktown*, the submarine *Clamagore*, and other fighting ships.

The first *Laffey* (DD459) cannot be visited. The destroyer lies now on the floor of Iron Bottom Bay (Sound), off Guadalcanal, her deep wounds hidden by 400 fathoms of murky water. "Instead of a bay, Iron Bottom is a 15-mile stretch of ocean between two main islands," said Bill Davis, who was aboard the *Laffey* on the fateful night of November 13, 1942. "They call it Iron Bottom because of all the ships that went down there."

During the fall of 1942, American and Japanese land, air, and naval forces engaged in a prolonged and bloody tug-of-war over the key island of Guadalcanal. "We had taken Guadalcanal in August of that year, and the Japanese were determined to take it back," said Davis. "We had already fought several [naval] actions in the area and got our tails whipped in every one of them."

Japanese torpedo bomber hits the water during combat near the Gilbert Islands on December 4, 1943. Note the pieces of the plane in the water.

Few ships ever survived a beating like the one taken by the *Laffey* on April 16, 1945, when the destroyer was hit by three bombs and five kamikaze planes. This is the ship's starboard side.

Japanese skippers and their crews had trained extensively at night and were expert at fighting in the dark. This gave the Imperial Navy a significant advantage at Guadalcanal, even though the Americans had radar and superior air cover. "They always came at us out of the dark," said Davis.

"On the night of Friday the 13th [November 13, 1942] it seemed like the whole Japanese Navy was coming at us. Suddenly a searchlight was in my face, and I fired at it with my 20mm. Bob Simms, in the 20mm mount next to mine, was also firing. The light was knocked out.

"Then a Japanese battleship [the *Hei,* which massively outweighed and outgunned the American destroyer] bore down on us. I thought she was going to cut the *Laffey* in half, but she just missed us—just barely. I was firing at the bridge of that battleship from no more than 75 feet away, and the rounds were chewing up the metal flash shield as if it were made of canvas. Then I was looking straight into the barrels of the big guns in the enemy's forward turret, and I thought right then I was going to die. But they weren't using their heavy guns to return our fire." The *Laffey* was so close to the *Hei* that the Japanese gunners could not lower their aim enough to hit the destroyer. "They were using their anti-aircraft and machine guns. A round struck the shield on my mount, but

I was okay. They missed me, but they got Simms. He was dead."

The *Laffey* fired torpedoes at the *Hei*. "We were so close they just bounced off without exploding." (Destroyer torpedoes armed themselves on the way to the target and would not explode unless they had traveled a certain distance in the water.) "I saw them jump right up out of the water when they hit the side of the *Hei*."

Soon the *Laffey* itself was hit with a torpedo fired by a Japanese destroyer. This one did explode. "I landed in a lifeboat on the other side of the ship. My shoes were gone."

The *Laffey* had been dealt a mortal blow. The blast ruptured the destroyer's fuel tanks, which instantly caught fire. The crew tried to fight the blaze but could not hold back the flames. Davis, now back on his feet, was standing within earshot of the *Laffey*'s skipper, Lieutenant Commander William Hank, when he gave the order to abandon ship. "Let's get the men off the ship," said Hank.

Davis was slow getting off the ship, until Hank spotted him. "Well! . . ." shouted Hank. "Go!"

"Aren't you coming, Captain?" asked Davis.

"Of course I'm coming," replied the skipper. Davis never saw him again.

Swimming away from the burning *Laffey* "at flank speed," Davis could taste oil in the water. He had just taken a foundering officer in tow when the Laffey's depth charges and magazines went up together in a tremendous blast. Then he saw the bow point skyward as his ship slid down to its grave. With her were fifty-six of the *Laffey*'s crew. But not Davis. On the following day he was rescued by a boat from Guadalcanal.

Several other American ships were sunk in this same action, known as the Battle of Guadalcanal. Hit by submarine torpedoes, the cruiser *Juneau* sank, carrying all but a few members of the crew with her. Among the dead on the *Juneau* were the five Sullivan brothers, for whom the destroyer *The Sullivans* was later named. Riddled by thirty-seven shells, the destroyer *Monssen* went down with a loss of 110 men. Another seventy-one officers and crew died when the heavily damaged destroyer *Cushing* sank. Cut in two by a pair of torpedoes, the destroyer *Barton* went down with 90 percent of her crew. Adding to the horror on this night of death, the destroyer *O'Bannon* ran through the splashing, gasping *Barton* survivors, sucking many of them into her screws.

The Japanese were also hurt. Several of their ships were heavily damaged or sunk. The worst loss was the *Hei*. The *Laffey* had done severe damage to its bridge and killed most of Vice Admiral Hiroaki Abe's staff. Abe himself was wounded. Like a cyclops with a sharp stake driven into its eye, the huge battleship stumbled blindly through the waves. Shortly before noon on the next day, bombers from Henderson Field on Guadalcanal caught up with the *Hei* and finished her. She went down stern first.

CHARLESTON, SOUTH CAROLINA

USS *Yorktown* (CV10)

Classification:	Aircraft carrier, Essex class (short-hull group)
Sister Ship:	*Intrepid* (CV11)
Crew:	380 officers, 3,088 enlisted men
Length:	888 feet
Beam:	147 feet
Draft:	Approximately 29 feet
Displacement:	27,100 tons (42,000 tons when fully loaded for combat)
Engines:	8 boilers
Power:	150,000 HP for maximum speed of more than 30 knots (35 mph)
Armament:	Antiaircraft guns (an assortment of 5", 40mm, and 20mm) Ninety planes Two launching catapults
Wartime Achievements:	Earned eleven Battle Stars and the Presidential Unit Citation
Nickname:	"Fighting Lady"

Named for the first *Yorktown* (CV5), which sank during the Battle of Midway in June 1942, the USS *Yorktown* (CV10) was built at the Newport News Shipbuilding and Drydock Company, in Newport News, Virginia. After being commissioned on April 15, 1943, the *Yorktown* served with the Pacific Fleet in action at Iwo Jima, Okinawa, the Philippines, Truk, and the Marianas. As one of the Navy's new "fast carriers," she set records for the fastest launches and recoveries of aircraft and the heaviest flying schedules.

The *Yorktown*'s guns shot down fourteen enemy planes, while her aircraft shot down 458 planes in the air and destroyed another 695 on the ground. The *Yorktown* received eleven battle stars for her outstanding wartime service.

The *Yorktown* continued to serve the Navy after the end of World War II, undergoing major modifications during the 1950s that added an angled deck for jets. Later she was converted into an antisubmarine carrier and participated in naval operations during the Vietnam War. In late December 1968 she was assigned to recover Frank Borman, James Lovell, William Anders, and their *Apollo 8* space capsule when they splashed down after their flight to the Moon.

The Navy decommissioned the *Yorktown* in 1970 and transferred

The magnificent *Yorktown* seems to sail through a sea of grass at Patriots Point.

her to the Patriots Point Development Authority as a memorial ship in 1975. Retaining her modified configuration but offering extensive World War II exhibits, the *Yorktown* is open to the public at Patriots Point Naval and Maritime Museum at Mount Pleasant, near Charleston, South Carolina.

Peering through sights like this one, 20mm and 40mm gunners on the *Yorktown* hammered away at Japanese bombers and kamikaze planes.

NOW HEAR THIS

The commanders of fighting ships posted daily messages to keep crew members mindful of their duties. On February 21, 1944, sailors on the *Yorktown* were warned: "We have started our run-in. From now on we will be operating within the estimated normal range of Japanese air searches. . . . When general quarters sounds, man your battle stations quickly and be fully ready to fight. . . . Keep your protective gear handy. . . you won't have time to look for it, and keep your shirt buttoned and your sleeves rolled down to protect against flash burns. On your toes!"

Some messages were more mundane, as when Executive Officer Cameron Briggs "chewed out" his crew for using too much fresh water: "20.3 gallons of fresh water per man was consumed yesterday and 19.9 gallons the day before. This amounts to a gallon per man over the allowance. Economize and make up the loss today, *or*—!"

A Douglas bomber prepares to roar down the deck of the _Yorktown_ for a raid on a Japanese-held island.

USS *Laffey* (DD724)

Classification:	Destroyer, Allen M. Sumner class
Crew:	350 officers and enlisted men
Length:	376 feet
Beam:	41 feet
Displacement:	2,200 tons
Engines:	4 boilers
Power:	Maximum speed of 36 knots (42 mph)
Armament:	Six 5" guns
	Twelve 40mm guns
	Eleven 20mm guns
	Ten torpedo tubes
Wartime Achievements:	Earned five Battle Stars and the Presidential Unit Citation

Gun barrels askew, the destroyer *Laffey* lies low in the water after being pounded by Japanese bombers and suicide planes.

Built by Bath Iron Works, in Bath, Maine, the USS *Laffey* bears the name of Bartlett Laffey, a seaman who earned the Civil War Medal of Honor, and of an earlier *Laffey* (DD459), which sank at the Naval Battle of Guadalcanal in 1942. After being commissioned on February 8, 1944, the destroyer bombarded German positions at Normandy in support of

the Allied landings on D-Day, June 6, 1944. The *Laffey* then joined the Pacific Fleet to participate in attacks on the Philippines, Tokyo, Iwo Jima, and Okinawa.

While working as part of a radar picket line off Okinawa on April 16, 1945, the *Laffey* withstood a seventy-nine-minute assault by twenty-two enemy planes. Although she shot down nine planes, five kamikazes and three bombs hit her, killing thirty-two men and wounding seventy-one. The *Laffey* received the Presidential Unit Citation for her brave and determined performance during this attack, and she earned five battle stars for other outstanding wartime service.

The *Laffey* continued to serve the Navy after the end of World War II. She participated in the atomic bomb tests at Bikini in 1946 and bombarded the coast of North Korea in 1953 during the Korean War. The Navy modernized her in 1962 and assigned her to missions in the Atlantic and the Mediterranean, where she served until she was decommissioned in 1975.

In 1981 the *Laffey* joined the *Yorktown* as a memorial ship at Patriots Point Naval and Maritime Museum, at Point Pleasant. Although she retains her 1960s modifications, the *Laffey* includes several World War II exhibits.

Patriots Point visitors today don't have to look too close to see the *Laffey*'s battle scars. At the left of the photograph is the stern of the submarine *Clamagore*.

USS *Clamagore* (SS343)

Classification:	Submarine, Balao class (modified into a Guppy III in 1948 and 1962)
Sister Ships:	*Batfish* (SS310), *Becuna* (SS319), *Bowfin* (SS287), *Ling* (SS297), *Lionfish* (SS298), *Pampanito* (SS383)
Crew:	8 officers, 72 enlisted men
Length:	311 feet 9 inches
Beam:	27 feet 3 inches
Draft:	15 feet 3 inches
Displacement:	1,526 tons (2,424 tons when submerged)
Engines:	4 diesel engines and 252 battery cells
Power:	20.25 knots (23 mph) maximum speed when surfaced; 8.75 knots (10 mph) when running on batteries while submerged
Armament:	Twenty-four torpedoes (ten torpedoes with fourteen reloads) Antiaircraft guns (an assortment of 5", 3", 40mm, and 20mm)

One of the U.S. Navy's last diesel-powered submarines, the USS *Clamagore* was built by the Electric Boat Company in Groton, Connecticut, and commissioned on June 28, 1945, about two months before the end of World War II. She spent her wartime tour of duty in the Atlantic and the Mediterranean.

Modifications in 1948 and 1962 converted the *Clamagore* into a Guppy III submarine. During her thirty years of service, the submarine operated out of Key West, Charleston, and New London, Connecticut. During the missile crisis in 1962 she patrolled the waters off Cuba.

The *Clamagore* was decommissioned on June 12, 1975, and was transferred to the Patriots Point Naval and Maritime Museum in 1981. The submarine retains her Guppy III configuration but includes World War II exhibits.

Resting beside the *Laffey*, the *Clamagore* invites visitors to go below decks to glimpse the confined living quarters of a submarine sailor.

USCGC *Ingham* (WHEC35)

Classification:	Coast Guard cutter
Sister Ship:	*Taney* (WHEC37)
Crew:	Approximately 120 officers and enlisted men
Length:	327 feet
Beam:	42 feet
Draft:	Approximately 13 feet
Displacement:	2,200–3,200 tons
Engines:	2 boilers
Power:	6,200 HP for 20 knots (23 mph) maximum speed
Armament:	Two 5" guns 40mm antiaircraft guns 20mm antiaircraft guns Two depth-charge tracks
Wartime Achievements:	Completed thirty-one convoy missions, participated in six amphibious operations, sank U-626

The USCGC *Ingham* (formerly the *Samuel D. Ingham*) was built by the Philadelphia Navy Yard, in Philadelphia. Commissioned in 1936, she was assigned to convoy duty during World War II, completing thirty-one missions in the North Atlantic, the Mediterranean, and the Caribbean. The *Ingham* is credited with sinking U-626.

Later in the war, the cutter was transferred to the Pacific, where she participated in six amphibious operations. In addition to her valuable service during World War II, the *Ingham* also served during the Vietnam War, earning the Presidential Unit Citation for outstanding performance.

The Coast Guard cutter was recently transferred to the Patriots Point Naval and Maritime Museum Association. The well-preserved *Ingham* is now open to the public for tours.

The handsome Coast Guard cutter *Ingham* saw more combat in World War II than many Navy ships.

CHAPTER FIVE

BIG GUNS ON THE BAMA

Appropriately, the license plate on Elmo Harris's yellow Dodge reads BB-60. Harris served on the USS *Alabama,* known to the U.S. Navy as BB-60, during that big battleship's entire fighting career. Today he lives in Pensacola, Florida, only about an hour's drive from the *Alabama*'s permanent berth in Mobile Bay. He makes the trip often.

"I was on her when she squeezed through the Panama Canal into the Pacific," said Harris. Squeeze is the right word. The *Alabama* has a beam of more than 108 feet, while the canal locks are only 110 feet wide. "It looked like we had about a foot of clearance on one side, but we had none at all on the other. We scraped right down the side of the lock. I figured that was just as well since we were due to scrape and paint that side anyway."

Harris's battle station was in the *Alabama*'s number-one turret. It fired 16-inch shells weighing 2,700 pounds, capable of disassembling any structure they hit. Harris said he once drove a Dodge Colt that weighed no more than the shells fired by each of the *Alabama*'s nine 16-inchers. The Colt, incidentally, was made in Japan.

With radar aiming and a range of 21 miles, the big guns could score precise hits on targets far over the horizon and devastate an enemy who could not even be seen. They were designed primarily for destruction of enemy ships. In order to wreak a maximum of havoc, their armor-piercing shells could penetrate far down into the bowels of a vessel before exploding. But, ironically, the *Alabama* never fired at a

The battleship *Alabama* at dusk

Japanese ship. As it turned out, the decisive sea battles of World War II were fought primarily with dive-bombers and torpedo planes flying from carriers often 100 miles or more from the enemy fleet. The 16-inchers were used frequently, however, to bombard islands and beaches before U.S. Marines stormed ashore.

According to Harris, when the big guns fired, the noise inside the turret was not so deafening as one might expect. "You felt a sudden violent lurch—the whole ship did—when those things went off. But all you heard was a sort of distant, rolling thunder. We were protected from the noise and from the enemy by 16 inches of steel armor."

The *Alabama*'s 20mm and 40mm antiaircraft guns were much harder on the ears of the men firing them than were the 16-inchers. Harris did not envy those men. Their guns were located above deck, where they were exposed to bullets and shrapnel, and their guns were in use far more often than his. The *Alabama* and other battleships were often used as giant antiaircraft platforms to protect the American fleet's fragile carriers.

Some of the 20mm guns on the *Alabama* still have the signs painted on their shields urging gunners to "LEAD, DAMMIT, LEAD." Like a hunter shooting at a flying duck, antiaircraft gunners had to fire out ahead of fast-moving enemy planes. Tourists who notice Harris's "Battleship *Alabama* Veteran" cap sometimes ask him about the sign. "You had to lead," he tells them, "otherwise the plane would be gone before the rounds reached it."

Decorations on the USS *Alabama*: The small Japanese flags represent beaches shelled (left) and aircraft downed (right). The color bars honor the battleship for the campaigns, operations, and battles in which it fought.

Harris makes sure visitors know his battle station was not one of the relatively small antiaircraft platforms that girded the ship. Proudly he leads them forward to his gun. Along the way, he is careful to point out the storeroom under the bridge where one of his shipmates operated an illicit whiskey still. "That was deadly stuff he brewed in there, made from potato peels and other scraps. The still threw up quite a smell, too. The captain was always complaining about the odor, but he never knew about the still."

At the mammoth number-one turret, Harris explains the firing procedure. Six 100-pound bags of high explosive were rammed into each of the three barrels and detonated to hurl at the enemy projectiles weighing "as much as a Toyota." And when the *Alabama* scored a hit? "Well, if you got hit by one of those things, it was fair to say you were having a bad day."

MOBILE, ALABAMA

USS *Alabama* (BB60)

Classification:	Battleship, South Dakota class
Sister Ships:	*South Dakota* (BB57), *Indiana* (BB58), *Massachusetts* (BB59)
Crew:	127 officers, 2,205 enlisted men
Length:	680 feet
Beam:	108 feet 2 inches
Displacement:	35,000 tons (43,000 tons when fully loaded for combat)
Engines:	4 engine rooms, each with boilers and 2 turbines
Power:	130,000 HP maximum, 28 knots (32 mph) maximum speed
Armament:	Nine 16" guns in three triple turrets (21 miles maximum range) Twenty 5" guns in ten twin mounts Forty-eight 40mm antiaircraft machine guns in twelve quadruple mounts Fifty-two 20mm single antiaircraft machine guns Three OS2U (Vought Kingfisher) aircraft Two launching catapults
Wartime Achievements:	Earned nine Battle Stars, the Navy Occupation Service Medal Pacific, and the Philippine Republic Presidential Unit Citation Badge; shot down twenty-two enemy planes, participated in ten bombardments of Japanese strongholds
Nickname:	"Lucky A"

Elmo Harris served on the *Alabama* throughout its fighting career. Nowadays Harris lives about an hour's drive from his old ship's permanent berth. He frequently makes the trip.

The USS *Alabama,* the fourth U.S. Navy ship to bear that name, was built at the Norfolk Naval Shipyard at a cost of approximately $77 million. After her commissioning on August 16, 1942, and shakedown training, the *Alabama* began her first tour of duty, serving with the North American Patrol Task Force 22 assigned to protect the aircraft carrier *Ranger.* Later she joined her sister ship *South Dakota* on Task Force 61 working with the British Home Fleet to guard lend-lease convoys running to the Russian port of Murmansk. In mid-1943 the *Alabama* and the *South Dakota* steamed through the Panama Canal and joined the Pacific Fleet at the New Hebrides Islands.

While in the Pacific, the *Alabama* earned nine battle stars for her outstanding service in the Gilbert Islands Operation (Tarawa invasion); the Marshall Islands Operation; the Asiatic-Pacific Raids (Truk, the Marianas, Palau, Yap, Ulithi, Woleai, Satawan, and Ponape); the Hollandia Operation (Aitape, Humboldt Bay, Tanahmerah Bay); the Marianas Operation (Saipan, Philippine Sea, Guam, Palau, Yap, Ulithi); the Western Caroline Islands Operation (Bonin, Yap, Palau, Philippines); the Leyte Operation (Okinawa, Luzon, Formosa, Visayas, Surigao Strait); the Okinawa Gunto Operation; and the Third Fleet Operations Against Japan.

In Operation Galvanic—the Gilbert Islands landings (November 19–December 8, 1943)—the *Alabama* helped screen the aircraft carrier *Yorktown,* using her antiaircraft batteries to drive off enemy aircraft. In Operation Flintlock in the Marshall Islands (January 29–February 8, 1944), the *Alabama* worked with other ships of the Fifth Fleet to destroy Japanese air power and shipping and joined with the *South Dakota* and the *North Carolina* in bombarding enemy positions at Namur. Serving as part of the *Bunker Hill* task group in the Asiatic-Pacific Raids (February 16–May 1, 1944) the *Alabama* helped destroy enemy aircraft, cruisers, destroyers, and other ships in the raid on Truk and screened U.S. aircraft carriers during strikes on the Mariana Islands. In the Hollandia Operation (April 21–24, 1944), the *Alabama* helped screen the aircraft carrier *Enterprise* and covered landings of General MacArthur's troops on the north coast of New Guinea.

The *Alabama* then sailed with the *Enterprise* task force in the invasion of the Marianas and fought in the Battle of the Philippine Sea. One of the few ships in the Pacific Fleet equipped with the new SK radar, the *Alabama* played a key role during the opening air battle in the Philippine Sea in detecting and destroying enemy aircraft, earning a commendation of "very well done" from the task force commander.

The *Alabama*'s enormous scale is especially apparent at night. The big ship's complete dominance of this scene is challenged only by a tiny wading bird at the bottom right of the photograph.

The *Alabama* assisted in the capture of Guam and also participated in Operation Stalemate II, the invasion of the Caroline and Palau islands (August 31–September 24, 1944). In the Leyte Operations (October 10–26, 1944), the *Alabama* screened aircraft carriers striking enemy positions in the Philippines, Formosa, the Pescadores, and the Ryukyu Islands.

After two years of continuous frontline service, the *Alabama* retired to the U.S. West Coast for an extensive overhaul. The battleship rejoined the Pacific Fleet in early May 1945 and, as part of the *Enterprise* task group, participated in Operation Iceberg, the invasion and occupation of Okinawa. The *Alabama* withstood the almost constant Japanese kamikaze attacks that made the battle to capture Okinawa the most costly and fierce of the war, and she also joined with other ships in the Third Fleet in bombarding targets on the mainland of Japan. Ultimately, the *Alabama* led the victorious column of American ships into Tokyo Bay.

In her three years of combat service, the *Alabama* suffered no crew casualties due to enemy fire, an almost miraculous feat that earned her the nickname "Lucky A." (Her only crew casualties were five crew members killed and eleven injured when a 5-inch gun accidentally fired during a nighttime assault in the Asiatic-Pacific Raids and one man lost overboard on another occasion.) The battleship was decommissioned on January 9, 1947, and placed in the reserve fleet at the Puget Sound Naval Shipyard, in Bremerton, Washington.

On June 1, 1962, the Navy struck the *Alabama* from its official list, but when the news reached the State of Alabama, a group of citizens spearheaded a drive to bring the ship to Mobile as a memorial. In July 1964 the Navy donated the ship to the state, and the USS *Alabama* Battleship Commission raised $1 million to cover the cost of towing the ship 5,600 miles from Bremerton to Mobile and establishing a permanent berth at a 100-acre park. The *Alabama* was dedicated and opened to the public on January 9, 1965.

If loaded, the *Alabama*'s battery of 5-inch guns could instantly annihilate the tank in the foreground or lay to waste the business district of Mobile a few miles away. During World War II, the 5-inchers were used mostly to throw up a "curtain" of antiaircraft fire.

USS *Drum* (SS228)

Classification:	Submarine, Gato class (fleet type)
Sister Ships:	*Cavalla* (SS244), *Cobia* (SS245), *Cod* (SS224), *Croaker* (SS246), *Silversides* (SS236)
Crew:	7 officers, 65 enlisted men
Length:	311 feet 8 inches
Beam:	27 feet 4 inches
Draft:	15 feet 3 inches
Displacement:	1,526 tons (2,410 tons when submerged)
Engines:	4 Fairbanks-Morse diesel engines and 252 battery cells
Power:	6,500 HP from diesel engines for 20 knots (23 mph) maximum speed when surfaced; 5 knots (6 mph) maximum speed when running on batteries while submerged
Armament:	Twenty-four torpedoes (ten torpedo tubes with fourteen reloads) One 5" gun One 40mm single-mount gun One 20mm twin-mount gun
Wartime Achievements:	Earned twelve Battle Stars; conducted thirteen war patrols; sank fifteen Japanese ships totaling more than 80,000 tons, the eighth highest of all U.S. submarines in total Japanese tonnage sunk

The 40mm gun at the left of the photograph was used mostly for antiaircraft fire. But the *Drum* and other submarines would rarely stand and fight back against an air attack. Instead, they would submerge as quickly as possible. While surfaced at sea, a submarine had no friends and, indeed, was likely to be attacked even by "friendlies."

Named for a large North Atlantic sea bass that makes a drumming noise, the USS *Drum* was built by the Navy Yard in Portsmouth, New Hampshire, at a cost of approximately $6.3 million. Commissioned on November 1, 1941, the *Drum* left the East Coast and headed toward Hawaii, arriving at Pearl Harbor on April 1, 1942. On her first war patrol (April 17–June 12, 1942), the *Drum* cruised the coast of Japan and sank the seaplane tender *Mizuho* and three cargo ships. After being refitted at Pearl Harbor, the *Drum* began her second war patrol (July 10–September 2, 1942) in the Truk area, where she damaged one enemy freighter.

While off the eastern coast of Kyushu on her

third patrol (September 23–November 8, 1942), the *Drum* sank three freighters and damaged at least two other ships. Her fourth patrol (November 29, 1942–January 24, 1943) included planting mines in the heavily traveled shipping channel at Bungo-suido. During this effort, the submarine damaged the fully loaded aircraft carrier *Rhuho* and a large tanker.

On her fifth patrol (March 24–May 13, 1943), the *Drum* searched the waters south of Truk and sank two freighters. After being refitted at Brisbane, Australia, the submarine undertook her sixth patrol near the Solomon Islands and Bismarck Archipelago (June 7–July 26, 1943), during which she sank the *Myoko Maru,* a cargo ship.

The submarine's seventh patrol (August 16–October 6, 1943) took her to the Admiralty Islands and along the north coast of New Guinea, where she sank a cargo ship. The *Drum* patrolled the Bismarck Archipelago and Caroline Islands during her eighth mission (November 2–December 5, 1943). The submarine sank an enemy cargo ship and attacked a convoy of four freighters, but a depth charge from one of the convoy's escorts heavily damaged the *Drum*'s conning tower, sending her home to the West Coast for repairs.

The *Drum* will never prowl the seas again. Today it serves as a museum and memorial to the World War II submariners who are "still on patrol."

The *Drum* returned to Pearl Harbor on March 29, 1944, and left eleven days later to patrol Iwo Jima and other islands in the Bonins (April 8–May 31, 1944). Although she did not attack any enemy targets, the *Drum* rescued two Japanese sailors from a sinking ship and gathered information that would be useful later in the U.S. bombardment of the islands.

Her tenth patrol (June 24–August 14, 1944) took the *Drum* to the Ulithi, Yap, the Fais Islands, and Peleliu, where she helped rescue downed airmen in the raids on Yap and Palau. During her eleventh patrol (September 9–November 8, 1944) the submarine cruised Surigao Strait for two weeks with no enemy contact and then moved to the South China Sea, where she patrolled during the Leyte landings and the battle for the Leyte Gulf and sank three Japanese cargo ships.

The *Drum* cruised to Nansei Shoto for her twelfth patrol (December 7, 1944–January 17, 1945) and then headed toward Guam without engaging any enemy ships. During her thirteenth patrol (February 11–April 2, 1945), the *Drum* worked with the *Piranha, Puffer,* and *Sea Owl* in a wolfpack called Bennett's Blazers. She participated in the assaults on Iwo Jim and Okinawa, providing lifeguard service for downed airmen, and then cruised to San Francisco for an overhaul.

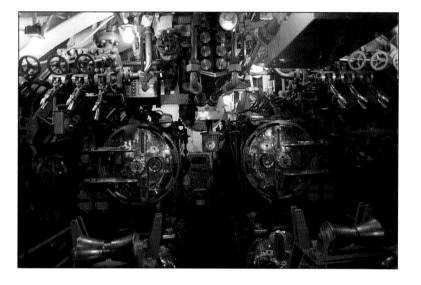

The *Drum* returned to Pearl Harbor in April 11, 1945, and was at Midway when the Japanese surrendered. She arrived home in Portsmouth, New Hampshire, in September 1945 and was decommissioned on February 16, 1946. From March 1947 through 1967, the *Drum* served in the Naval Reserve program at Washington, D.C.

The *Drum* once carried twenty-four torpedoes, enough to keep these well-polished torpedo tubes busy and to sink several enemy ships if the captain was lucky and his eye sharp.

The submarine was assigned to the inactive fleet at Norfolk, Virginia, in 1967 and remained there until the Navy donated her to the USS *Alabama* Battleship Commission in April 1969. The *Drum* was towed to Mobile in May 1969 and opened to the public in dedication ceremonies on July 4, 1969.

The USS *Alabama* and USS *Drum* are open daily (except Christmas) at Battleship Memorial Park on U.S. Route 90 (Battleship Parkway) off Interstate 10 in Mobile. Visitors are invited to follow self-guided tour routes through both ships. The *Alabama* also features displays dedicated to the highly decorated destroyer USS *Evans* and the cruiser USS *Mobile*. The park offers numerous exhibits, including Corsair and Hellcat "Mustang" WWII fighter planes; the "Calamity Jane," a B-52 bomber that served in the Strategic Air Command (SAC); and a Redstone rocket.

A DAY OF PEACE: CHRISTMAS 1943

Elmo Harris, aboard the battleship *Alabama* in the New Hebrides Islands:

"I had recently gotten a big fruitcake from back home, and I decided this was the day to eat it. A Marine—I don't remember his name—brought up a half gallon of vanilla ice cream. I can't imagine where he got it. I guess he stole it. The Marine pulled out his bayonet and used it to spread the ice cream on pieces of fruitcake as we passed them out to the guys. It was the craziest thing. There we were, 10,000 miles from home, celebrating Christmas with ice cream and fruitcake."

Jack Killough, aboard the submarine *Drum* in the South Pacific:

"We had just crossed the equator. We took tin foil, pieces of colored wire and string, and everything we had and hung it up to make it look like Christmas. Let me tell you, there was nothing commercial about this Christmas. It was the real thing, a truly spiritual Christmas. I don't think I've ever had a better one. We had baked ham for dinner, sang songs, and tried to imagine what it was like at home."

Robert Benson, aboard a PT-boat in the Solomon Islands:

"They gave us pretty good chow that day—turkey, dressing, you name it. That day was easy to remember because we didn't have to eat mutton. We were close to Australia, and every day we ate mutton this and mutton that. Have you ever had mutton hash for breakfast? You could throw that stuff away—we usually did—and even the birds wouldn't eat it."

Christmas dinner aboard the *Yorktown:* celery hearts, stuffed olives, sweet pickles, cream cheese, tomato juice, turkey consommé, soda crackers, roast turkey, cornbread dressing, baked ham with prune sauce, creamed peas and carrots, asparagus salad, hot raisin rolls, French apple pie, hard Christmas candies, cigars, and cigarettes.

The *Alabama* fires its 16-inch guns. These huge guns delivered a hefty punch, their shells weighing 2,700 pounds and capable of devastating any target they struck.

CHAPTER SIX

AN OCEAN ON FIRE

"The first submarine I ever saw was the *Nautilus,* and to tell you the truth, I wondered what the hell it was."

Before the war, Jack Killough served on the battleship *Oklahoma.* But by the time the war began, Killough had been transferred to the USS *Permit,* a submarine. So, as fortune would have it, he was not aboard the *Oklahoma* when the Japanese bombed and sank her at Pearl Harbor. Killough knew some of 415 men killed on the *Oklahoma* that day. "I was what you might call a lucky fellow," he said.

Although Killough had been on the *Permit* in the Philippines when the war started (see pages 7–9 for more about Killough's experiences on the *Permit*), he was later assigned back to Honolulu. "They thought I had an ulcer."

Tests showed he did not have an ulcer, but by that time, the *Permit* was already far out in the Pacific hunting down Japanese freighters, and the Navy gave Killough a desk job at Pearl Harbor. Four months later a friend named Harlan Gibbs dropped in to say goodbye.

"Gibbs said he was shipping out on the *Drum.* He was pretty unhappy about it, since he had a wife in Honolulu. Well, I told him it was a shame I couldn't go in his place."

Later the captain of the *Drum* approached Killough and asked him if he was serious about his offer to go to sea in place of Gibbs. Kil-

Hit by torpedoes from the *Drum*, a Japanese cargo ship goes down. The photograph was taken through the *Drum*'s periscope.

lough said he was. "I was sure nothing would come of it, but the fact is, I ended up shipping out and Gibbs stayed behind at Pearl."

The *Drum*'s skipper, Mike Rindscopft, appointed Killough Chief of the Boat (C.O.B.). The chief functioned as the captain's right-hand man, especially in personnel matters. "For instance, the chief assigned the bunks," said Killough. "For that and other reasons the C.O.B. was known to some of the men as the S.O.B."

Rindscopft was a very young captain. During one of the *Drum*'s extended patrols, Killough and some of the other crewmen organized a surprise party to help Rindscopft celebrate his twenty-sixth birthday. Despite his youth, however, Rindscopft proved a highly successful and efficient submarine captain. During a run north of the Philippines, the *Drum,* with Rindscopft in command, sank seven ships in less than two days.

"We'd been finding dead American fliers in life rafts. The Japanese had cut their heads off and dumped their heads on top of their feet. I guess they thought that would frighten us.

"We were following a convoy. We tracked that bugger for three days, waiting for the right moment to hit them, and then there came a perfect night. No moon. No stars. The captain decided to run in on the surface. We fired all six of our forward torpedoes, wheeled around, and fired four out of our stern tubes. When those torpedoes started going off, it was like we'd hit a fireworks factory. It looked like the whole ocean was on fire."

Only seconds after this picture was taken, the kamikaze plane near the top of the frame crashed into the destroyer *Kidd*. The attack off Okinawa on April 11, 1945, killed thirty-eight of the *Kidd*'s crew, including the photographer who took this picture.

BATON ROUGE, LOUISIANA

USS *Kidd* (DD661)

Classification:	Destroyer, Fletcher class
Sister Ship:	*The Sullivans* (DD537), *Cassin Young* (DD793)
Crew:	20 officers, 309 enlisted men
Length:	376 feet 5 inches
Beam:	39 feet 7 inches
Draft:	Approximately 18 feet
Displacement:	2,050 tons (2,940 tons when fully loaded for combat)
Engines:	4 boilers, 2 steam-geared turbines, 2 turbo generators
Power:	35.2 knots (approximately 41 mph) maximum speed
Armament:	Five 5" guns Three to five 40mm antiaircraft guns Twelve 20mm antiaircraft guns Five 21" torpedo tubes in quintuple banks Six depth-charge projectors (K-guns) Two depth-charge tracks
Wartime Achievements:	Earned four Battle Stars, the Philippine Liberation Medal, and the World War II Victory Medal
Nickname:	"Pirate of the Pacific"

Antiaircraft gunners often strapped themselves into a harness like the one shown below on the destroyer *Kidd*.

The USS *Kidd* was built at the Federal Shipbuilding and Drydock Company in Kearny, New Jersey, at a cost of $6 million. The destroyer bears the name of Rear Admiral Isaac Campbell Kidd, who was commanding his flagship, the *Arizona*, when a bomb hit the bridge and a magazine explosion sank the ship during the Japanese attack on Pearl Harbor, December 7, 1941. Admiral Kidd was posthumously awarded the Medal of Honor and the Purple Heart, and his widow christened the *Kidd* in his honor on February 28, 1943.

In addition to the name of a U.S. Navy commander, the destroyer also bears the name of seventeenth-century pirate William Kidd, whose image was painted on her forward stack. True to the courage and daring exhibited by these two men, the *Kidd* earned four Battle Stars for her outstanding wartime service.

Commissioned on April 23, 1943, the destroyer escorted aircraft carriers in the Atlantic and Caribbean and patrolled shipping lanes off Newfoundland until August 1943, when she was assigned to escort the battleships *Alabama* and *South Dakota* through the Panama Canal to Pearl Harbor. In late September and early October 1943, the *Kidd* escorted aircraft carriers in preparation for the assault on Wake Island. During the last half of October 1943, she served as one of nine destroyers assigned to screen the carriers *Essex, Bunker Hill,* and *Independence* in the attack on Rabaul. While rescuing U.S. airmen downed during that strike, the *Kidd* fought off attacks by enemy aircraft, shooting down three Japanese planes.

The destroyer also provided support for U.S. troops landing on Bougainville and for the invasion of Tarawa in the Gilbert Islands Operation (November 19–23, 1943). During the Marshall Islands Operation in late January and February 1944, the *Kidd* screened U.S. ships, escort-

The *Kidd* rests at Baton Rouge, Louisiana. Because of their relatively light armor and construction, destroyers were sometimes called "tin cans" by the sailors who served on them.

ed minesweepers into the waters off Majuro, and participated in the bombardment of beaches.

From March 20 until April 14, 1944, the destroyer stood guard off the coast of Emirau while U.S. troops built an airfield on the island, and then she provided support for the occupation of Aitape and Hollandia in New Guinea. In June and July 1944, the *Kidd* participated in the operations to secure Saipan and the attacks on Guam. She returned to Pearl Harbor in late August for repairs.

Rejoining the Pacific Fleet at Eniwetok in late September 1944, the *Kidd* participated in the Leyte Operations against enemy strongholds in the Philippines, Formosa, the Pescadores, and the Ryukyu Islands. In mid-December 1944, the destroyer left the front line of battle and steamed to the U. S. West Coast for a major overhaul, which lasted until February 10, 1945.

The *Kidd* returned to the Pacific theater in mid-March 1945 and bombarded the island of Okinawa in support of U.S. landings there. During this mission, the destroyer patrolled as part of the radar picket line screening other ships in Task Force 58 of the Fifth Fleet. Her duties included rescuing downed airmen, fighting off kamikaze attacks, destroying mines, and providing the other ships with early warning of enemy attack. On April 11, 1945, a kamikaze plane struck the *Kidd*, killing thirty-eight men, wounding more than fifty others, and tearing a breach in the hull at the forward fireroom. Despite the extensive damage, the ship's crew restored the *Kidd*'s speed to twenty-five knots within three minutes of the attack, an amazing feat that saved the destroyer from further damage. After temporary repairs at Ulithi, the *Kidd* returned home to the West Coast.

In addition to major repairs while in the San Francisco Navy Yard, the destroyer also underwent a major modification that upgraded her fire-control system, antiaircraft guns, and radar equipment. The *Kidd* left the West Coast for Pearl Harbor on August 20, 1945, about two weeks before the Japanese surrendered. At the end of September 1945 the destroyer returned to San Diego and was placed in the Pacific Reserve Fleet.

The *Kidd* was recommissioned on March 28, 1951, to serve in the Korean War. During the late 1950s and early 1960s, the destroyer completed a series of cruises in both the Pacific and the Atlantic. Beginning in April 1962, she served with the Naval Destroyer School at Newport, Rhode Island, until she was again decommissioned and placed on reserve on June 19, 1964. The Louisiana Naval War Memorial Commission obtained possession of the ship in 1982.

Now carefully restored to her 1945 configuration and wartime camouflage appearance, and resting on a unique cradle that allows her underwater structure to be seen when the Mississippi River is at low level, the *Kidd* is open to the public at the foot of Government Street on the river in Baton Rouge. The site also includes the Nautical Historic Center.

A rope and tackle and other equipment on the *Kidd*

USS *Texas* (BB35)

Classification:	Battleship, Texas class
Crew:	98 Navy officers, 2 Marine officers, 1,625 enlisted Navy men, 82 enlisted Marines
Length:	573 feet
Beam:	106 feet
Draft:	28 feet 6 inches
Displacement:	30,355 tons (34,000 when fully loaded for combat)
Engines:	6 boilers and 2 turbines
Power:	20.4 knots (24 mph) maximum speed
Armament:	Ten 14" guns Six to fourteen 5" guns Ten 3" guns Ten 40mm guns Sixteen to forty-four 20mm guns Three OS2U Kingfisher aircraft One launching catapult
Wartime Achievements:	Earned five Battle Stars and the Navy Occupation Service Medal, Pacific
Nickname:	"Mighty T"

One of the oldest ships to serve in the U.S. Navy during World War II, the USS *Texas* was built by the Newport News Shipbuilding and Drydock Company, in Newport News, Virginia, and commissioned on March 12, 1914. Before the outbreak of World War I, the *Texas* served with the U.S. fleet in the Atlantic and the Caribbean. During that war, she completed Allied patrol missions in the North Sea. The battleship was part of the warship convoy that witnessed the surrender of the German fleet at the entrance to the Firth of Forth on November 21, 1918.

The *Texas* was refitted and modernized at the Norfolk Navy Yard between 1925 and 1927, and during the 1930s she served as the flagship of the U.S. Fleet. When World War II broke out in Europe in 1939, the *Texas* was assigned to serve in the Neutrality Patrol, which escorted neutral shipping in the North Atlantic. After the Japanese attack on Pearl

Harbor and the entrance of the United States into the war in December 1941, the battleship escorted convoys transporting U.S. troops to Europe, Africa, and the Panama Canal Zone.

The *Texas* earned her first battle star for her support services during the Algeria-Morocco landings, part of the North African Occupation (November 8–11, 1942). In 1943 the battleship again provided essential escort duties for convoys to Casablanca, Morocco, Gibraltar, Scotland, and Ireland.

The *Texas*'s outstanding service on D-Day (June 6, 1944) and during the invasion of Normandy (June 6–25, 1944), including the bombardment of German-held Cherbourg, earned the ship her second battle star. As flagship of the Omaha Beach bombardment task force, the *Texas* fired more than 1,100 rounds of ammunition at German

A true old-timer, the battleship *Texas* dates from 1914, before World War I. In fact, the ship served with distinction in both wars. In spite of its age, the *Texas* proved its mettle off Normandy by "softening" German positions before and after D-Day (June 6, 1944).

strongholds. During the attack on Cherbourg, a direct enemy hit destroyed the battleship's navigation bridge, injuring more than ten crew members and killing the helmsman, the *Texas*'s only crew fatality of the war.

After her damage was repaired, the *Texas* joined Allied forces supporting the invasion of southern France (August 15–September 28, 1944). Her invaluable service in shore bombardment and assault on enemy batteries earned the ship her third battle star.

In late September 1944 the *Texas* returned to New York to be repaired and refitted for war missions in the Pacific. In December 1944 she steamed through the Panama Canal to join Task Force 52 at Ulithi Atoll in preparation for the invasion of Iwo Jima (February 16–March 7, 1944). Her outstanding performance in bombarding Japanese strongholds during the assault and occupation of the island earned the *Texas* her fourth battle star.

The battleship's next assignment was to serve in the assault and occupation of Okinawa (March 25–May 14, 1945). In the week before the U.S. landings, the *Texas* participated in shore bombardments and minesweeping operations. In action for a period of fifty days, her crew fired the equivalent of four shiploads of ammunition (2,019 rounds of 14-inch shells, 2,640 rounds of 5-inch shells, and 5,865 rounds of smaller-caliber shells) and fought off heavy Japanese air assaults, including kamikaze attacks. The battleship was awarded her fifth battle star for this excellent performance.

After completing her mission at Okinawa, the *Texas* withdrew to the Leyte Gulf, where she received word of the Japanese surrender. The battleship cruised to Okinawa in late August 1945 and, after embarking veterans, left for California, arriving at San Pedro on October 15, 1945. The *Texas* made three more "Magic Carpet" round-trips between California and Pearl Harbor, bringing more than 4,000 U.S. veterans back home.

The Navy decommissioned the battleship from wartime service on October 27, 1945, and moved her to the reserve fleet at Norfolk in February 1946. The citizens of Texas saved the ship from scrapping by raising the money needed to prepare a permanent berth and cover the cost of towing her from Virginia to Texas. The state of Texas obtained possession of the battleship, and she arrived at San Jacinto Battleground Park, near Houston, on April 21, 1948, the anniversary of Texas's independence from Mexico.

The USS *Texas* underwent extensive restoration from late 1988 through the summer of 1990. The battleship, the last of the "Dreadnoughts" and the only surviving ship to have fought in both World Wars, is open to the public Wednesday through Sunday at her berth at the San Jacinto Battleground Park.

This photograph of the *Texas* under fire by a German shore battery (June 25, 1944) was autographed by Admiral Chester A. Nimitz.

C.W. Nimitz,
Fleet Admiral, USN

USS *Stewart* (DE238)

Classification:	Destroyer escort, Edsall class
Crew:	216 officers and enlisted men
Length:	306 feet
Beam:	36 feet 10 inches
Draft:	12 feet 3 inches
Displacement:	1,200 tons (1,490 tons when fully loaded for combat)
Engines:	Diesel engines
Power:	6,000 HP, 19.5 knots (23 mph) maximum speed
Armament:	Three 3" guns
	Three 21" torpedo tubes
	Antiaircraft guns (an assortment of 20mm and 40mm)
	K-guns
	Depth charges
Wartime Achievements:	Successfully completed approximately thirty escort missions

A pair of 20mm guns on the destroyer *Stewart*

Built at Brown Shipbuilding Company in Houston, Texas, the USS *Stewart* bears the name of Rear Admiral Charles Stewart, who commanded the USS *Constellation* from 1805 to 1813 and the USS *Constitution* ("Old Ironsides") from 1813 to 1815 during the War of 1812. The destroyer escort is the second ship named for the admiral. The first *Stewart,* a World War I destroyer (DD224), has the somewhat embarrassing distinction of being the only major U.S. ship to serve in the Japanese Navy during World War II. The destroyer was in drydock on Java when the Japanese invaded the island in March 1942. Retreating U.S. troops tried to scuttle the ship, but the Japanese were able to save and refit her, slightly altering her appearance. At the end of the war the U.S. Navy recovered the ship at Honshu, Japan, and towed her to Pearl Harbor, where she was recommissioned into service as the USS *Ramp* (Recovered Allied Military Property).

The destroyer escort *Stewart* was commissioned on May 31, 1943, and spent almost her entire wartime career in the Atlantic. Designed to screen other ships from enemy submarine, surface, and air attack, the *Stewart*, and other destroyer escorts, primarily served to escort convoys of merchant vessels and warships. In addition to screening ships across the waters of the North Atlantic, the *Stewart* also served as a "school" ship, carrying student Navy officers on training cruises in the Caribbean.

In late June 1945, the *Stewart* and two other destroyer escorts, the *Edsall* and the *Moore*, transitted the Panama Canal to San Diego. Leaving the West Coast in late July, the three ships reached Pearl Harbor on August 4, 1945, for training in preparation for the planned U.S. invasion of Japan. The *Stewart* was still in training when the Japanese surrendered. Three days after the formal peace treaty was signed, the destroyer escort left for San Diego, arriving with war veterans aboard on September 12, 1945.

Even though the *Stewart* was not awarded any battle stars, her wartime service is noteworthy. The destroyer escort successfully completed about thirty convoy missions through North Atlantic waters infested with German submarines. None of her crew was killed during the war, and only one man was seriously injured.

After the war the *Stewart* served in the reserve fleet home-ported in Philadelphia until she was decommissioned at the end of 1945. Stricken from the official register and scheduled to be scrapped in 1972, the destroyer escort was purchased for $1.00 by the state of Texas and the Seawolf Commission. The USS *Stewart*, thought to be the last destroyer-escort in existence, is open to the public at Seawolf Park, in Galveston.

The *Stewart*, shown here at Galveston, Texas, held one wartime distinction that many ships' crews would have envied. Not a single *Stewart* sailor was killed during the war.

USS *Cavalla* (SS244)

Classification:	Submarine, Gato class
Sister Ships:	*Cobia* (SS245), *Cod* (SS224), *Croaker* (SS246), *Drum* (SS228), *Silversides* (SS236)
Crew:	7 officers, 65 enlisted men
Length:	Approximately 312 feet
Beam:	Approximately 27 feet
Draft:	Approximately 15 feet
Displacement:	Approximately 1,500 tons (more than 2,400 tons when submerged)
Engines:	4 diesel motors and 252 battery cells
Power:	6,400 HP from diesel engines for 20.25 knots (23 mph) maximum speed when surfaced; 8.75 knots (10 mph) maximum speed when running on batteries while submerged
Armament:	Twenty-four torpedoes (ten torpedo tubes with fourteen reloads) One 4" gun One 40mm single-mount gun
Wartime Achievements:	Earned four Battle Stars, the Presidential Unit Citation, and the Navy Occupation Service Medal, Pacific; completed six war patrols; sank 34,180 tons of Japanese shipping, including the aircraft carrier *Shokaku*
Nickname:	"The Luckiest Ship in the Submarine Service"

The USS *Cavalla* is launched on November 14, 1943. It and many other submarines were built by the Electric Boat Company of Groton, Connecticut.

Named for a family of spiny-finned fish, the USS *Cavalla* was built by the Electric Boat Company in Groton, Connecticut, and commissioned on February 29, 1944. After completing her shakedown training off the East Coast, the submarine cruised through the Panama Canal, reaching Pearl Harbor on May 9, 1944. The *Cavalla* spent her entire wartime career in the Pacific, earning battle stars for her outstanding performances in the Marianas Operation (Battle of the Philippine Sea, June 19–20, 1944), the Western Caroline Operation (capture and occupation of the southern Palau Islands, September 6–October 14, 1944), the Third Fleet Operations Against Japan (July 10–August 15, 1945), and Submarine War Patrol (November 14, 1944–January 13, 1945). She also earned a Presidential Unit Citation for her patrol of the eastern Philippine area from May 31 to August 3, 1944.

During her first war patrol (May 31–August 3, 1944) in the waters off the east coast of the Philippines, the *Cavalla* sighted a large Japanese task force. Instead of picking a target and attacking, the submarine risked becoming a target herself by tracking the enemy ships as they cruised toward Saipan. The *Cavalla* was therefore able to gather valuable information that helped U.S. forces in the Battle of the Philippine Sea.

On June 19, 1944, the submarine sighted another enemy task force consisting of two heavy cruisers, three destroyers, and a fully-loaded aircraft carrier. The *Cavalla* hit the carrier with three torpedoes, scoring a major victory—the sunk vessel, the *Shokaku,* was one of Japan's two largest aircraft carriers, a 30,000-ton ship that had taken part in the attack on Pearl Harbor. Even though the remaining enemy ships dropped more than 100 depth charges on the submarine, the *Cavalla* escaped serious damage and was able to reach Saipan for repair and refueling.

After being refitted at the island of Majuro during August 1944, the *Cavalla* worked with other submarines in a scouting line to intercept enemy ships during the U.S. invasion of Palau (September 6–October 14, 1944). The submarine then retired to Fremantle, Australia, for refitting and training before beginning her third war assignment, patrolling the South China and Philippine seas. During that patrol, she sank two freighters and a destroyer.

On her fourth war patrol, the *Cavalla* operated in the South China Sea and the waters off French Indochina. Although the submarine did not find any suitable enemy targets, she successfully avoided damage from enemy aircraft bombs, mines, and a submarine torpedo.

Her fifth patrol took the *Cavalla* to the Java Sea on lifeguard duty. No airmen were downed during the time of her mission, but she escorted the damaged British submarine *Terrapin* to Fremantle for repairs. The Japanese surrendered during the submarine's sixth patrol, and she proceeded to Tokyo Bay for the signing of the peace treaty onboard the *Missouri* on September 1, 1945. After refueling at Pearl Harbor, the submarine transitted the Panama Canal and arrived at New London, Connecticut, on October 6, 1945.

The *Cavalla* was decommissioned from wartime service in January 1946 and remained in retirement until April 10, 1952, when she was recommissioned to serve with Submarine Squadron 10. In 1952 she was converted to a hunter-killer configuration with a streamlined sail, an extended and squared bow, and modern electronic tracking equipment. The *Cavalla* continued to serve in the U.S. Navy until she was decommissioned on December 30, 1969. The U.S. Submarine Veterans WWII Association of Texas obtained possession of the ship on January 21, 1971, and moved her to Seawolf Park in Galveston. The restored submarine opened to the public for tours on April 11, 1971.

USS *Stewart* and USS *Cavalla* are permanently berthed (on dry land) at Seawolf Park, a manmade island on the Houston Ship Channel at Galveston. The park, which is dedicated to the memory of the USS *Seawolf* (SS197) and submariners lost during World War II, includes other military exhibits as well.

The *Cavalla* looks as if it took a wrong turn and sailed right up onto land. A memorial ship is easier and less expensive to maintain on land, and, of course, there is no danger of it sinking.

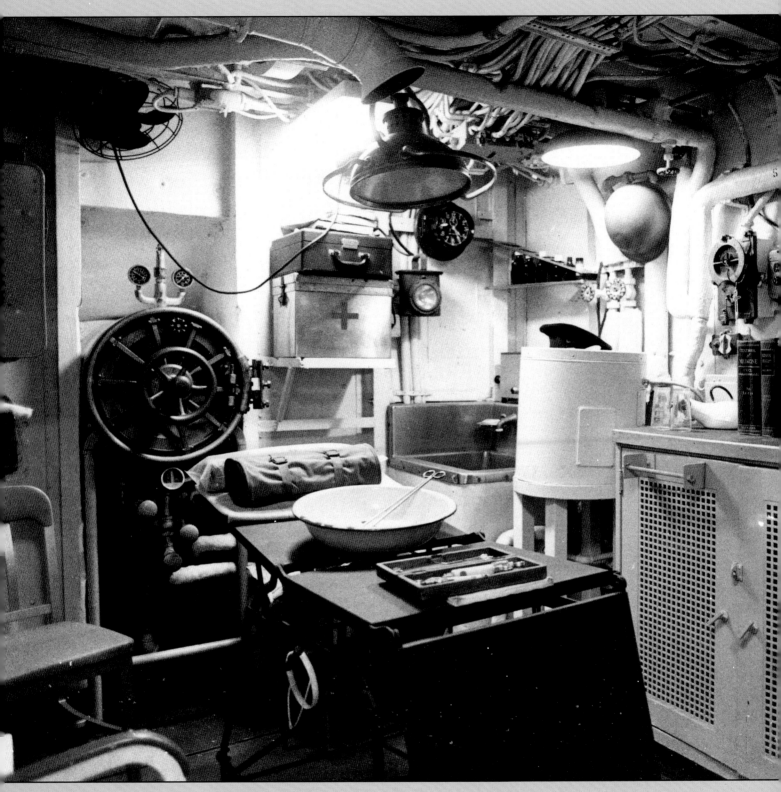

Spartan but practical — a typical shipboard medical facility

CHAPTER SEVEN

THE GOOD SHIP *SOLACE*

During World War II, Roger Griffith spent twenty-eight months on a naval vessel and visited some of the hottest combat zones in the Pacific, yet he never fired a shot at the Japanese. His ship never shelled an enemy-held beach, shot down an airplane, or sent a torpedo racing toward some doomed tanker. Unlike the Navy's other ships, Griffith's vessel did not observe blackout at night to avoid the notice of prowling submarines. In fact, it shined powerful lights on its hull, which was painted white for easier recognition by the enemy. Despite all of this, Griffith and his ship survived the war with barely a scratch and both could boast an enviable war record.

Griffith's war experience was unlike that of many World War II sailors because he served on the USS *Solace* (AH-5). Known formerly as the *Iroquois,* this unusual vessel had been a luxury passenger liner making runs between New York, Florida, and Cuba. With the coming of war, however, its elegant staterooms and lounges were converted for use as wards and operating rooms, and the *Iroquois* became the *Solace,* a hospital ship. "Our mission was to save lives, not to take them," said Griffith. "We were proud of what we did."

As a deck and communications officer, Griffith had little to do with the medical functioning of the ship—the hours-long operations needed to pull pieces of shrapnel out of a young pilot's chest or rebuild a Marine's shattered face. All of that was left to a team of surgeons and nurses. "They were good, very good," said Griffith. "You could not have gotten better care in any hospital in the United States."

As U.S. combat forces moved from island to island, from one battle to the next, the *Solace* followed. Seriously wounded sailors, Marines, and soldiers were brought aboard, treated, and later ferried to land-based hospitals. Then the *Solace* returned for another load of battered and bleeding warriors.

Although the *Solace* was often close to the fighting and exposed to many of the same dangers as warships, it had no protective armament of any kind. No military supplies were allowed on board. "We were not allowed to carry so much as a bag of mail from one port to another."

Even wars have rules. The combatants in World War II agreed not to attack one another's hospital ships so long as they carried no military cargo. Generally speaking, the prohibition was respected by both sides. Japanese submarines are known to have photographed the *Solace*, indicating they could have torpedoed the ship but had refrained from violating their agreement.

The U.S. hospital ships were painted white with a large red cross on each side to distinguish them from fighting ships and freighters. Nonetheless, the *Solace* was bombed at least once. "The attack came when we were about an hour out of Okinawa," said Griffith. "The plane dropped two bombs, but luckily they straddled us. One bomb exploded off the port and the other off the starboard."

The *Solace* also had a close call with a kamikaze bomber, again off Okinawa. "He came right down at us, and for a moment we were sure he would hit us. There was nothing to stop him, but he missed us and went into the water off our port bow. We fished him out."

Apparently the pilot had mistaken the *Solace* for a warship and recognized his error just in time to veer off. "Over the years, I've wondered about that," said Griffith. "Maybe he had made a mistake. But at the time, most of us thought he had decided to go on living. If that was it, then he certainly picked the right place to ditch." The crew of the *Solace* rescued the pilot, and his injuries were treated on the same ship his bomber might have destroyed.

As communications officer, Griffith often participated in conferences where battle plans were discussed. "They told us what to expect. For instance, if the terrain was uneven and our troops would be moving up hill, we would prepare for a lot of head and shoulder wounds."

Although Griffith seldom came under enemy fire while aboard the *Solace*, he saw plenty of combat action on shore. "I was on the beach at Saipan," he said. "Shells keep slamming into the sand, and they were not ours."

When U.S. forces stormed the beaches of the important Japanese-held island of Saipan, they had immediately come under intense mortar and artillery fire. "We were pinned down," said Griffith, who crouched in the tiny U.S. toehold on the island, radioing messages to medical teams waiting on the *Solace*. "We were sending boatloads of wounded out to the ship, and I would call and tell them what was coming."

Relentless shelling from U. S. warships had obliterated a major

Saipan sugar refinery near the Marine beachhead, but a tall, black smokestack had been left standing for use as a navigation marker. "Nobody could figure out why the enemy fire was so deadly accurate until somebody discovered a Japanese observation post up there in the stack. Once our guys knocked out that post, things settled down a bit, but until they did, things were plenty hot for us."

Griffith, nevertheless, had his most harrowing day of the war aboard the *Solace*. After the ship's navigator fell ill, the captain collared his communications officer and said, "Mr. Griffith, you are now the navigator."

"I'd had training," said Griffith, "but no experience whatsoever with navigation. I swallowed hard and became the navigator. The worst of it was, I had to take us through a coral reef down near New Guinea. We had to make a very tight turn to get past the reef, and I can tell you, I was scared to death."

The *Solace* and Griffith came through the reef unscathed. After more than two years aboard the hospital ship, Griffith was transferred to a tanker. He was married three days after the Japanese surrender and spent his last months of active duty running a small Navy hotel at Fort Monroe, in Old Point Comfort, Virginia.

The officers' wardroom on the destroyer *Kidd*

CLEVELAND, OHIO

USS *Cod* (SS224)

Classification:	Submarine, Gato class
Sister Ships:	*Cavalla* (SS244), *Cobia* (SS245), *Croaker* (SS246), *Drum* (SS228), *Silversides* (SS236)
Crew:	8 officers, 72 enlisted men
Length:	311 feet 9 inches
Beam:	27 feet 3 inches
Draft:	15 feet 3 inches
Displacement:	1,526 tons (2,424 tons when submerged)
Engines:	4 diesel engines and 252 battery cells
Power:	22 knots (26 mph) maximum speed when surfaced; 9 knots (10 mph) maximum speed when running on batteries while submerged
Armament:	Twenty-four torpedoes (ten torpedo tubes with fourteen reloads) One 5" gun Two 20mm guns
Wartime Achievements:	Earned seven Battle Stars, one for each of her wartime patrols; officially credited with sinking 26,985 tons of enemy shipping; unofficially credited with sinking more than forty ships, many of which were less than the 500-ton criterion for official recognition

Named for the cod family of fish, the USS *Cod* was built by the Electric Boat Company in Groton, Connecticut. The submarine was commissioned on June 21, 1943, and sent to the Western Pacific. Operating out of ports in Australia and the Philippines, the *Cod* successfully completed all seven of her wartime patrols and earned the unique distinction of being awarded a battle star for each one of her patrols. Although the *Cod* reported having sunk forty enemy vessels, Navy records credit her with fewer ships because some of her targets were less than the 500-ton minimum for official recognition. Officially the submarine sank 26,985 tons of enemy shipping, including a destroyer.

At the end of the war, the Navy placed the *Cod* in the reserve fleet, where she remained until recommissioned for service in the Korean War. In 1959 the submarine moved to Cleveland, Ohio, to serve as a training ship for submarine reservists.

The Navy decommissioned the submarine on December 15, 1971, and donated her to the Cleveland Coordinating Committee for Cod as a memorial ship. The *Cod* is open to the public at the Naval Reserve Center, off North Marginal Drive between East Ninth Street and Burke Lakefront Airport on Lake Erie. The only World War II submarine to retain her hatch and ladders (instead of being modified with stairs), the well-preserved *Cod* allows visitors to tour her entire interior, including her torpedo rooms.

The *Cod* as it looked just after World War II

USS *Silversides* (SS236)

Classification:	Submarine, Gato class (fleet type)
Sister Ships:	*Cavalla* (SS244), *Cobia* (SS245), *Cod* (SS224), *Croaker* (SS246), *Drum* (SS228)
Crew:	8 officers, 72 enlisted men
Length:	312 feet
Beam:	27 feet
Draft:	Approximately 15 feet
Displacement:	1,525 tons (2,410 tons when submerged)
Engines:	4 diesel engines and 252 battery cells
Power:	Approximately 20 knots (23 mph) maximum speed when surfaced; 8–9 knots (10 mph) maximum speed when running on batteries while submerged
Armament:	Twenty-four torpedoes (ten torpedo tubes with fourteen reloads) Antiaircraft guns (an assortment of 3", 4", and 20mm)
Wartime Achievements:	Earned twelve Battle Stars and a Presidential Unit Citation, conducted fourteen war patrols, sank twenty-three Japanese ships (the third highest number of ships sunk by any U.S. submarine) for a total tonnage of more than 90,080 tons (the fifth highest of any U.S. submarine in total Japanese tonnage sunk)

Built at Mare Island Naval Shipyard, in Vallejo, California, the USS *Silversides* was commissioned on December 15, 1941, just eight days after the Japanese attacked Pearl Harbor. Assigned to the Pacific Fleet, the *Silversides* completed fourteen war patrols in the East China Sea and the waters off the coast of Japan, the Marianas, the Carolines, Bismarck Archipelago, the Solomons, and Guadalcanal. Assigned to interrupt the flow of oil, food, iron ore, and other supplies to Japan, the submarine sank a total of twenty-three vessels, totaling more than 90,080 tons of shipping.

In addition to patrol duties, the *Silversides* also participated in minelaying and reconnaissance missions, and, serving with the Submarine Lifeguard League, she rescued American pilots downed in air strikes on Japan. In her long and distinguished wartime career, the *Silversides* suffered only one crew casualty, an impressive record that led her to be called a "lucky boat."

The *Silversides* bears the dubious distinction of being the only U.S. submarine to "fly" the Japanese flag while in battle. This embarrassing and somewhat dangerous incident occurred when she was making a run on an enemy ship and accidently snared some Japanese fishing nets bearing the rising sun symbol. An enemy patrol boat spotted her while she was struggling to get rid of the entangling trappings. Her vital element of surprise destroyed, the *Silversides* was forced to abandon the attack.

The *Silversides* attacks a Japanese sampan with its deck gun.

Another one of the *Silverside*'s wartime experiences has been retold in several movies, including *Destination Tokyo*. While the ship was submerged beneath an enemy vessel off the coast of New Ireland in the Bismarck Archipelago, the submarine's pharmacist's mate performed an emergency appendectomy on a crew member. Even though the operation was done with makeshift instruments and neither the "surgeon" nor the volunteer "surgical team" had any surgical experience, the patient not only survived but was back on duty less than a week later.

When the war ended, the *Silversides* returned to the United States and was towed up the Mississippi River to the Naval Reserve Armory at Chicago. The submarine served as a reserve training ship from October 1947 until the Navy decommissioned and struck her from the official register on June 30, 1969.

The Great Lakes Navy Association was formed in 1972 to save the famous submarine from being scrapped. The Navy sold the ship to the association in July 1973, and she was moved to her current berth at Muskegon, Michigan, in 1987. Almost completely restored to her World War II specifications, the *Silversides* is open to the public at Pere Marquette Park, on the shores of the channel between Lake Michigan and Muskegon Lake.

MANITOWOC, WISCONSIN

USS *Cobia* (SS245)

Classification:	Submarine, Gato class (fleet type)
Sister Ships:	*Cavalla* (SS244), *Cod* (SS224), *Croaker* (SS246), *Drum* (SS228), *Silversides* (SS236)
Crew:	8 officers, 72 enlisted men
Length:	Approximately 311 feet
Beam:	Approximately 27 feet

Draft:	Approximately 15 feet
Displacement:	1,525 tons (2,424 when submerged)
Engines:	4 diesel engines and 252 battery cells
Power:	Approximately 21 knots (24 mph) maximum speed when surfaced; 9 knots (10 mph) maximum speed when running on batteries while submerged
Armament:	Twenty-four torpedoes (ten torpedo tubes with fourteen reloads) One 3" gun One 20mm antiaircraft gun One 40mm antiaircraft gun
Wartime Achievements:	Earned four Battle Stars, conducted six war patrols, sank thirteen Japanese ships totaling more than 18,000 tons (including vessels ranging from a small junk to a 7,800-ton cargo ship)

The USS *Cobia* was built by the Electric Boat Company in Groton, Connecticut, at an inclusive cost of approximately $6.3 million. Commissioned on March 29, 1944, the submarine joined the Pacific Fleet and undertook her first war patrol on June 16, 1944. On July 13, 1944, she scored her first hit, sinking a 2,800-ton Japanese storeship.

In a running surface battle during her fourth patrol, the *Cobia* sank two more large enemy ships but suffered her first and only crew casualty. Official records, which include only destroyed vessels weighing 500 tons or more, credit the *Cobia* with sinking 16,835 tons of enemy shipping. If her smaller hits are included, the *Cobia* sank more than 18,000 tons.

In 1946 the navy placed the submarine in the reserve fleet, where she remained until she was recommissioned in 1951 to serve as a training ship. The *Cobia* was on reserve again from 1954 until 1959 when she began eleven years of service as a training ship for the submarine reserves of Milwaukee.

A group of citizens in Manitowoc formed an association in 1968 to spearhead a drive to bring a submarine to their city as a memorial to the twenty-eight submarines built there during World War II. The *Cobia* was stricken from the Navy's official list of ships in 1970 and was towed to Manitowoc. Dedicated on August 23, 1970, as a memorial to all submariners and to the people who constructed the Manitowoc submarines, the *Cobia* is now open to the public at the Manitowoc Maritime Museum. In addition to the restored submarine, the museum site also includes a display of model ships and maritime exhibits.

USS *Hazard* (AM240)

Classification:	Minesweeper, Admirable class (fleet type)
Crew:	8 officers, 90 enlisted men
Length:	184 feet 6 inches
Beam:	33 feet 4 inches
Displacement:	625 tons (945 tons when fully loaded for combat)
Engines:	2 900-HP Cooper-Bessemer locomotive diesels
Power:	15 knots (approximately 17 mph) maximum speed
Armament:	One 3" gun
	Two 40mm antiaircraft guns in twin mounts
	Six 20mm antiaircraft guns in twin mounts
	Two depth-charge projectors (K-guns)
	Two depth-charge racks
	One (Mark 10) "Hedgehog"
Wartime Achievements:	Earned three Battle Stars

The steel-hulled minesweeper USS *Hazard* was built by the Winslow Marine Railway Company in Winslow, Washington. Equipped to perform patrol, radar-picket, convoy escort, antisubmarine, and mine-clearing duties, the *Hazard* was commissioned on October 31, 1944, and then completed two months of shakedown training. The minesweeper began her wartime service on January 5, 1945, when she left San Francisco escorting a convoy to Pearl Harbor.

For the next two months, the *Hazard* screened convoys cruising from Pearl Harbor to Eniwetok Atoll and the Philippines. Assigned to Rear Admiral Ingolf Kiland's task force during the invasion of Okinawa (March 14–June 30, 1945), the *Hazard* served on antisubmarine patrols and swept up the mines around Kerama Retto, a demanding task that took almost three months to complete.

The *Hazard* next served in a massive minesweep operation in the East China Sea, northwest of Okinawa. On July 14, 1945, she returned to Buckner Bay and remained on standby until August 13, when she rejoined a minesweeping unit in the East China Sea.

After the Japanese surrendered, the *Hazard* cleared the waters and screened the way for several occupation convoys cruising to Korea and Japan. With her wartime assignments completed in late November 1945, the *Hazard* returned to the West Coast, reaching San Diego in time for Christmas. Transitting the Panama Canal, she arrived in Galveston in February 1946. The Navy decommissioned the minesweeper and placed her in the mothball fleet at nearby Orange, Texas, where she remained for the next twenty-five years.

In 1971 the Greater Omaha Military Historical Society, a group of businessmen, purchased the *Hazard,* refurbished the ship, and had her pushed by towboat from Orange up the Mississippi and Missouri rivers to Omaha. The largest ship to travel so far inland, the *Hazard* coursed the 2,000 miles in twenty-nine days. The minesweeper, now restored as a World War II memorial and museum, is permanently berthed on the shore of the Missouri River.

The USS *Hazard* is open to the public at Freedom Park, on Abbott Drive off Interstate 480 in east Omaha. In addition to tours of the minesweeper, the park also offers exhibits of equipment from other ships, a Douglas A4D "Skyhawk" carrier jet, a single-mount turret for a 5-inch gun, and tours of the USS *Marlin* (SST2), a 131-foot training/target submarine completed in 1953.

Compared with other branches of the military, the Navy has long maintained a reputation for good chow, such as that once busily prepared in the galley on the *Kidd*.

USS *Batfish* (SS310)

Classification:	Submarine, Balao class
Sister Ships:	*Becuna* (SS319), *Bowfin* (SS287), *Clamagore* (SS343), *Ling* (SS297), *Lionfish* (SS298), *Pampanito* (SS383)
Crew:	8 officers, 72 enlisted men
Length:	312 feet
Beam:	27 feet
Draft:	Approximately 15 feet
Displacement:	1,526 tons (approximately 2,400 when submerged)
Engines:	4 diesel engines and 252 battery cells
Power:	20 knots (23 mph) maximum speed when surfaced; approximately 10 knots (12 mph) when running on batteries while submerged
Armament:	Twenty-four torpedoes (ten torpedo tubes with fourteen reloads) Antiaircraft guns (an assortment of 5" and 40mm)
Wartime Achievements:	Earned nine Battle Stars and a Presidential Unit citation, sank three submarines (in a period of only four days) and eleven other ships for an official total of 10,558 tons (an unofficial total of more than 37,000 tons) of enemy shipping
Nickname:	"America's sub killer"

The USS *Batfish* was built at the Portsmouth Naval Shipyard, in Portsmouth, New Hampshire, and was commissioned on May 5, 1943. Named for a ferocious fish found in the waters of the West Indies, the submarine proved her aggressiveness by sinking three enemy submarines in a period of four days, February 10–13, 1945. In addition to the enemy submarines, the *Batfish* sank a Japanese destroyer in August 1944 and seven other ships, for an official total of 10,558 tons of enemy shipping (the *Batfish* claims an unconfirmed total of 37,080 tons).

After the *Batfish* was stricken from the official Navy register in 1969, six barges attempted to tow the submarine up the Arkansas River to Tulsa. Unable to navigate the sharp turn in the river at Muskogee, the ship was secured in the shallow water at the edge of the river channel. Next, a 2,000-foot canal was dug for the ship and separated from the river by dikes. Finally, the water was pumped from the canal. Permanently beached, the *Batfish* is open to the public as part of War Memorial Park, off the Muskogee Turnpike in Muskogee. Tours of the submarine include an audiotape that recreates the sounds of World War II life aboard the ship. The park also contains a monument dedicated to the submarine *Shark* (SS174), which was sunk in 1942; bronze memorials bearing the names of fifty-two submarines and their crew members lost during the war; and a museum.

To most visitors who did not serve on them, and to many of the sailors who did, World War II submarines all look the same below decks—cramped and uninviting.

Among the last surviving Liberty Ships, the *Jeremiah O'Brien* holds a berth at San Francisco Bay. No one ever called them handsome, but the Liberties helped win the war.

CHAPTER EIGHT

UGLY DUCKLINGS

With the opening of World War II, Germany unleashed one of history's most fearsome naval forces—the U-boat. Operating in "wolf packs," these silent killers hunted down and destroyed ships with relentless efficiency. Strategic rather than tactical weapons, they seldom attempted to engage and sink warships of the powerful British Navy. Instead, they sought to throttle their enemy by cutting off the flow of food, fuel, and supplies to the British Isles. To do this, they preyed almost exclusively on hapless merchant vessels. During the first nine months of the war alone, they sank more than 150 vessels, over one million tons of shipping. Soon the prowling wolf packs were sinking freighters much faster than the British could build or replace them.

Long before the United States entered the war as an active combatant, President Franklin Delano Roosevelt had pledged America's support in Britain's struggle against the Axis powers. Until Pearl Harbor, however, that help came mostly in the form of war materials—and the ships needed to freight them across the Atlantic. To replace the shipping tonnage destroyed by German torpedoes—and to prepare for the day when America might also be forced to fight—Roosevelt launched the most intensive shipbuilding effort the world has ever seen.

At first, U.S. shipyards sought to fill the flood of government orders with relatively sophisticated vessels, but the British were crying out for "ships built by the mile and chopped off by the yard." To meet the demand for quantity, builders were forced to adopt the mass-production techniques already made famous by the American automobile industry. Plans were drawn up for a simple, medium-sized freighter that could be built quickly. The result was the Liberty Ship, a practical and sturdy, if inelegant, vessel.

When the first of more than 2,751 of these "emergency" vessels hit the water, newspapers immediately dubbed them "ugly ducklings." They had blunt bows and lines that could hardly be described as graceful. Even Roosevelt said they were "dreadful-looking objects."

Naturally enough, certain design compromises had been necessary. The new ships had welded hulls and were powered by old-fashioned triple expansion engines rather than turbines. Top speed—with a following wind—was eleven knots. Most navigating was done from what was euphemistically called a "flying bridge," actually a small, exposed station atop the forecastle. There the helmsman, captain, and other bridge officers braved all but the worst of weather before retreating to the low wheelhouse, where visibility was so poor they risked slamming into unseen rocks, or worse, some other half-blind Liberty. Accommodations for the officers and crew were spartan. Even the captain's cabin was small. He was afforded a tiny head and shower of his own, but few other amenities of any sort.

"They were not pretty or luxurious, but you could take one across the Atlantic and back again," said Ralph Albers, who served as radio officer on the *Charles Poston, Nathan Davis,* and several other Liberty Ships during the war. "And you could carry a lot of cargo—beans, bombs, or barbed wire—anything that was needed."

Liberty Ships had a displacement of 4,000 tons, but could carry 10,000 tons of cargo—two-and-one-half times their own weight. This made them tempting targets for the enemy, and with their slow speed, the lumbering Liberties were especially vulnerable to attack. Partly for that reason, they were designed to be three-quarters freighter and one-quarter warship. They even had armor, although very unlike the heavy steel plates that girded the Navy's combat ships. Certain parts of the ship were protected by a thick layer of a material not unlike asphalt and often referred to as "plastic armor." Most Liberties were also fitted with at least one 5-inch, up to three 3-inch, and as many as eight 20mm guns. Usually the guns were manned by regular navy gunners who lived aboard ship in quarters separate from those of the merchant seamen.

"Sometimes those [guns] were put to good use," said Albers. Several Liberties fought off attacks by submarines. The *Stephen Hopkins* actually sank the *Steir,* a heavily armed German commerce raider. The *John Brown*—now under restoration in Baltimore—fought a daylong duel with German guns in the hills above Anzio, in Italy.

Still, many Liberties succumbed to attack. Enemy bombs, shells, and torpedoes sank more than 200 with a loss of nearly 7,800 lives. But most got through, running tanks and ammunition through icy Arctic seas to Soviet Murmansk, delivering airplanes and aviation fuel to remote island airfields in the Pacific, ferrying troops to Britain to prepare for the D-Day invasion.

All of this was possible, not because the Liberty Ships were well designed or well constructed but because they could be (and were) built in a hurry. The first Liberties, built in 1941, each took about seven months to complete; but by the middle of the war, shipyards were cranking them out in less than a week. It should be noted that during the war American workers also turned out warships, tanks, airplanes, and other instruments of war in prodigious quantities. For instance, the Japanese, who had faced six American fleet carriers at the beginning of the war, were forced to contend with more than thirty by war's end.

The push to turn out ships and other wartime necessities created a new kind of war hero—the production worker. Nearly every American knew that "Rosie the Riveter" built Liberty Ships. So successful was the legendary Rosie and her fellow workers, many of them women, that from eighteen separate shipyards they were able to launch 2,751 Liberties in only about four years. Lined up bow to stern, these ships would form a bridge more than 230 miles long, or approximately the distance between New York and Baltimore. The British call for ships "built by the mile" had been answered. In fact, if every Liberty built had been gathered at Dover, they could have formed a solid causeway more than ten ships wide across the British Channel to France. The enormous productivity of American shipyards filled Allied ports all over the world with the boxy Liberties. The arms and materials the ubiquitous ugly ducklings delivered piled up into hills, then into mountains, overwhelming the Axis powers and hastening the day that Albers and millions of others like him will never forget.

"We were at sea when the message came in," said Albers. "I thought I'd better go and tell the captain. He was one of those hard-as-nails types. His name was S. M. Foster, he must have been at least eighty years old, and I believe he had actually been a sailing ship captain up in New England. I'm not sure I ever saw the skipper smile."

Albers would not see his old skipper smile on this day, either. "Sir," said Albers, leaning for support against the solid steel frame of the door to Foster's cabin. "Sir, I thought I'd better tell you. The war is over."

There was only a hint of a pause.

"Oh, the war's over, you say," said Foster in a gruff voice. "Well, I guess you'd better put a notice on the bulletin board for the men."

In World War II, Liberty Ships carried war supplies to every theater of operations. They sailed in tropic heat and arctic cold to deliver everything from tanks and planes to beer and cigarettes to the fighting fronts. During America's island-hopping Pacific campaign, Liberty Ships took part in landings from Guadalcanal to Okinawa.

Liberty Ships were an emergency response to a shortage of cargo ships at the start of the war. Using a standard design and mass production techniques, U.S. shipyards were able to build a Liberty in only eight weeks.

Of 2751 look-alike Liberty Ships, only this one survives in its original state. The *Jeremiah O'Brien* is moored here at the former San Francisco Port of Embarkation and is open to the public.

A plaque on the *O'Brien*

SAN FRANCISCO, CALIFORNIA

USS *Pampanito* (SS383)

Classification:	Submarine, Balao class
Sister Ships:	*Batfish* (SS310), *Becuna* (SS319), *Bowfin* (SS287), *Clamagore* (SS343), *Ling* (SS297), *Lionfish* (SS298)
Crew:	10 officers, 70 enlisted men
Length:	311 feet 8 inches
Beam:	27 feet 3 inches
Draft:	15 feet 9 inches
Displacement:	1,525 tons (2,415 tons when submerged)
Engines:	4 diesel engines and 252 battery cells
Power:	23 knots (27 mph) maximum speed when surfaced; 11 knots (13 mph) maximum speed when running on batteries while submerged
Armament:	Twenty-four torpedoes (ten torpedo tubes with fourteen reloads) One 20mm antiaircraft gun One 40mm antiaircraft gun
Wartime Achievements:	Earned six Battle Stars, completed six wartime patrols, officially credited with sinking five enemy ships for a total of 27,288 tons, rescued seventy-three British and Australian POWs

Built at the naval shipyard in Portsmouth, New Hampshire, the USS *Pampanito* was commissioned on November 6, 1943. She served with the Pacific Fleet during World War II, completing six patrols and fighting in more than a dozen major battles. Official records credit the submarine with sinking five enemy ships, totaling 27,288 tons, and damaging four others. The *Pampanito* unofficially claims to have sunk six vessels.

During the *Pampanito*'s third war patrol, she worked with the USS *Growler* (SS215) and the USS *Sealion II* (SS315). The three submarines attacked a Japanese convoy on September 12, 1944, sinking seven of the eleven ships. Unknown to the submarine captains, two of the sunken ships, the *Rakuyo Maru* and the *Kachidoki Maru,* were carrying British and Australian prisoners of war. When the *Pampanito* returned to the area of the attack three days later, she found the surviving POWs in makeshift rafts. The *Pampanito* picked up seventy-three of the POWs and called in three other U.S. submarines to help with the rescue operations.

After the end of the war, the *Pampanito* served as a training ship for the Naval Reserve until she was decommissioned on December 20, 1971. The National Maritime Museum Association of San Francisco obtained possession of the submarine in May 1976 and opened her to the public on March 15, 1982, at Pier 45 on Fisherman's Wharf.

The *Pampanito* in San Francisco

SS *Jeremiah O'Brien* (Liberty Ship)

Classification:	Liberty Ship
Sister Ship:	*John W. Brown*
Crew:	81 men
Length:	Approximately 441 feet
Beam:	Approximately 57 feet
Draft:	Approximately 28 feet
Displacement:	Approximately 14,000 tons
Engines:	Reciprocating steam engine
Power:	2,500 HP for maximum speed of 11 knots (13 mph)

Named for an Irish-American sea captain who fought against the British in the American Revolution, the SS *Jeremiah O'Brien* was built by the New England Shipbuilding Corporation, in South Portland, Maine. After being launched on June 19, 1943, the Liberty Ship embarked on her maiden voyage from Boston to the United Kingdom.

Like her sister Liberty Ships, the *O'Brien* made numerous voyages carrying supplies and troops to ports in South America, Europe, Australia, and the Pacific. In June and July 1944 she made eleven round-trips between the British coast and Normandy in support of the D-Day invasion of France.

On February 7, 1946, the *O'Brien* was withdrawn from active service and scheduled to be converted into a hospital ship, but she remained for the next thirty-three years and eight months with the National Defense Reserve Fleet, at Suisun Bay, California. In 1966 plans were made to save the *O'Brien,* one of only a few Liberty Ships to have escaped scrapping. It wasn't until June 1979, however, that restoration work began on the ship. On October 6, 1979, the *O'Brien* steamed out of the reserve fleet and into the Bethlehem Steel shipyard at San Francisco for major overhaul. On May 21, 1980, she participated in her first Annual Seamen's Memorial Cruise and arrived at her new home berth at Pier 3 in the Golden Gate National Recreation Area, where she is now open to the public as a museum ship.

A Liberty Ship could carry up to 10,000 tons of war material and other cargo. Here the empty *Jeremiah O'Brien* rides high in the water.

USS *Arizona* (BB39)

Classification:	Battleship, Pennsylvania class
Sister Ship:	*Pennsylvania* (BB83)
Crew:	2,555 total officers and enlisted men
Length:	608 feet
Beam:	106 feet 3 inches
Draft:	Approximately 34 feet
Displacement:	33,100 tons
Engines:	6 boilers
Power:	32,000 HP maximum, 21 knots (24 mph) maximum speed
Armament:	Twelve 14" guns Twelve to sixteen 5" guns Three planes Two launching catapults

Built by the New York Naval Yard, the USS *Arizona* was commissioned on October 17, 1916. The battleship served as a gunnery training ship and patrolled off the East Coast during World War I. After the war ended, the *Arizona* became the flagship of the Atlantic Fleet and later worked with several battleship divisions in the Pacific.

On December 7, 1941, the *Arizona* was anchored in Pearl Harbor. Japanese torpedoes and bombs struck the battleship during the early-morning surprise attack, killing 1,103 of her crew and sinking the ship. The Navy did not refloat the *Arizona* after the attack but left her resting on the bottom of the harbor and flew the American flag from her superstructure, which remained above water. In 1962 the Navy covered the hull of the sunken ship with a 184-foot enclosure, which now houses a museum, assembly area, and a memorial to the men who lost their lives aboard the battleship.

Before the storm: The battleship *Arizona* blasts through high waves off the California coast. The *Arizona* and the nation's other "battlewagons" were expected to provide a bulwark against Japanese attack.

USS *Bowfin* (SS287)

Classification:	Submarine, Balao class
Sister Ships:	*Batfish* (SS310), *Becuna* (SS319), *Clamagore* (SS343), *Ling* (SS297), *Lionfish* (SS298), *Pampanito* (SS383)
Crew:	8 officers, 72 enlisted
Length:	312 feet
Beam:	27 feet
Draft:	Approximately 15 feet
Displacement:	1,526 tons (2,414 tons when submerged)
Engines:	4 diesel engines and 252 battery cells
Power:	20.25 knots (23 mph) maximum speed when surfaced; 8.75 knots (10 mph) maximum speed when running on batteries while submerged
Armament:	Twenty-four torpedoes (ten torpedo tubes with fourteen reloads) Antiaircraft guns (an assortment of 4", 40mm, and 20mm)
Wartime Achievements:	Earned eight Battle Stars, the Presidential Unit Citation, and the Navy Unit Commendation; completed nine war patrols; officially credited with sinking sixteen enemy ships, ranking her fifteenth in vessels sunk and seventeenth in tonnage sunk

Named for an iridescent predatory freshwater fish, the USS *Bowfin* was built by the Portsmouth Naval Shipyard, in Portsmouth, New Hampshire. The submarine was commissioned on May 1, 1943, and served with the Pacific Fleet during World War II. She completed nine war patrols, supported U.S. troop landings in the Philippines, participated in lifeguard duty to rescue downed American airmen, and laid mines.

Official records credit the *Bowfin* with sinking sixteen enemy vessels, ranking her fifteenth in the number of ships sunk and seventeenth in tonnage sunk. The submarine claims a total of forty-four vessels sunk, totaling 179,946 tons—totals that would place the *Bowfin* first of all U.S. submarines in both categories. The *Bowfin* also sank a bus, a unique feat that occurred when she destroyed a floating dock during the assault on Japan near the end of the war.

In addition to earning eight battle stars, the *Bowfin* was one of only five submarines to earn both the Presidential Unit Citation and the Navy Unit Commendation. After the war ended, the submarine served with the Atlantic Fleet until she was decommissioned on December 1, 1971. Now maintained by the Pacific Fleet Submarine Memorial Association, the *Bowfin* is open to the public at Pearl Harbor.

The Balao class submarine *Bowfin* is on display at Honolulu.

The USS *Arizona* Memorial is built above the remains of a proud ship and of the men who died on her.

DEATH OF A STEEL MASTODON

On April 6, 1945, the battleship *Yamato* raised its mighty anchors and put to sea one last time. Before the ship left sight of land, the entire 2,767-man crew received a ration of sake for a solemn, silent toast. None of these sailors expected to see Japan again, for this was to be their final battle.

Among the heaviest and most powerful warships ever constructed, the *Yamato* displaced more than 64,000 tons of seawater, making it half again heavier than the typical American battlewagons—the *North Carolina* displaced only about 44,000 tons, even when fully loaded for combat. The *Yamato*'s primary turrets held 18-inch guns—as compared to 16-inch guns on the *North Carolina*—which could obliterate targets up to 25 miles away with shells weighing more than a ton. Despite its heavy armament and enormous displacement, the big ship could knife through the water at twenty-six knots.

As the pride of the Japanese Navy, the *Yamato* had served as Admiral Yamamoto's flagship during the Battle of Midway. But unlike some capital ships, it was a fighter—not just an oversized office for an admiral. In the Philippines, it had charged like a rogue elephant, trampling and scattering a small American fleet off Samar. Throughout the war, the *Yamato*'s speed and devastating punch made it a threat the U.S. Navy could never ignore. Looming large in battle after battle, it had seemed invincible.

But now the *Yamato* was hopelessly outnumbered. More than three years of bombing, shelling, torpedoing, and depth-charging had sent nearly all of the once vast Japanese fleet to the bottom of the Pacific. By the spring of 1945, when the Americans invaded Okinawa, the Imperial Navy's greatest battleship stood almost alone.

From the point of view of the Japanese, the struggle for Okinawa was the most important battle of the war. Operating from airfields on this key island, B-29 bombers could reach every major Japanese city. In a desperate attempt to stop or at least slow the invasion, the Imperial high command ordered the *Yamato* to attack the U.S. fleet.

The Japanese Admiralty and the crew of the *Yamato* understood this was to be a one-way mission, no less suicidal than the plunge of a kamikaze bomber onto the deck of a cruiser. Only enough fuel was pumped into the battleship's huge tanks to carry it to Okinawa. Fuel for a return trip was considered unnecessary. "Our time is up," Captain Nomura told his men. "But let *Yamato*, the Divine Wind, live up to her name."

Naturally, the Japanese hoped their bold attack would catch the Americans by surprise, but this was not to be. A U.S. submarine lurking off the south coast of Japan spotted the *Yamato* and its small escort fleet of battered destroyers as they steamed out of the Inland Sea. The submarine skipper decided not to attack, but reported the course and speed of the enemy fleet to his superiors off Okinawa.

By midday on April 7, the *Yamato* had covered half the distance to Okinawa, and to that point the voyage had proceeded without incident. The somber mood that had gripped the ship earlier began to lighten. Officers on the bridge were promised a special treat for their evening meal—shiruko, sweetened red bean soup served with rice cakes. "His Majesty's" brand cigarettes were passed out to the entire crew.

Few if any of the cigarettes had been smoked when, shortly after noon, an ominous roar was heard out over the ocean. Moments later, a swarm of more than 100 U.S. carrier planes swooped down out of the east. The *Yamato* blazed away at the Americans with more than 150 machine guns and dozens of larger antiaircraft pieces. For nearly a quarter of an hour the battleship zigzagged crazily, successfully dodging every attack, but finally a torpedo slammed into its port side. Although far from fatal, the damage slowed the *Yamato*, allowing 500-pound bombs and other torpedoes to find their target. Fresh waves of attackers, striking 100 or more at a time, darkened the sky with their wings. Machine-gun bullets swept the bloodied decks clear of sailors. Engines slowed, the rudder jammed, and compartments flooded, causing an ever increasing list. Finally, twisted beyond recognition by the explosions of seventeen bombs and twenty torpedoes, the *Yamato* began its inevitable slide into the Pacific.

Realizing the *Yamato* was finished, the ship's senior officers quietly shook hands, said farewell to old friends, and retired to their cabins to wait for the rising water. Stunned ensigns tried to tie themselves to the binnacle or other objects to ensure that they too would go down with the ship. Seeing this, the *Yamato*'s aging chief of staff flew into a rage. Punching and kicking his junior officers to bring them to their senses, he shouted his last order. "Into the water and swim, all you young men."

Minutes later, the *Yamato* had gone to the bottom, leaving a scattering of debris on the surface and a few men struggling desperately to keep their heads above the oily water. Down with the *Yamato* went more than 1,000 giant shells, each one of which might have sunk an American ship. Down also went 2,498 sailors, more than 90 percent of the crew. Although attempts were made to save the ship's treasured portrait of Emperor Hirohito, it was never seen again.

Helldiver bombers race toward Japanese targets on Iwo Jima, February 22, 1945.

During World War II, sailor Jack Killough would sit here to talk over problems on the *Drum* with his captain. Nowadays Killough regularly visits the submarine and sits in this same spot "just to think things over."

Appendix

For more information regarding the ships profiled in this book,
contact the appropriate organizations listed below.

Ship	Organization	Address	Telephone
USS *Cassin Young*	National Park Service	National Historical Park Boston, MA 02129	(617) 223–5200
USS *Massachusetts* USS *Lionfish*	Battleship Cove	Fall River MA 02721	(800) 533–3194 (out of state) (800) 660–MASS (in state) (508) 678–1100 (local)
USS *Intrepid*	Intrepid Sea-Air-Space Museum	Pier 86 West 46th Street and 12th Avenue New York, NY 10036	(212) 245–0072
USS *The Sullivans* USS *Croaker* USS *Little Rock*	Buffalo Naval and Servicemen's Park	1 Naval Park Cove Buffalo, NY 14202	(716) 847–1773
USS *Ling*	Submarine Memorial Museum	Box 395 Hackensack, NJ 07602	(201) 342–3268
USS *Becuna*	Cruiser Olympia Association	Penn's Landing Delaware Avenue and Spruce Street Philadelphia, PA 19106	(215) 922–1898
USS *Torsk* USS *Taney*	Baltimore Maritime Museum	Pier III Pratt Street Baltimore, MD 21202	(301) 369–3854

A burial at sea: These officers and men of the aircraft carrier *Intrepid* died during a kamikaze attack off Okinawa on November 25, 1944. Today's memorials honor these men and others like them.

Ship	Organization	Address	Telephone
SS *John W. Brown*	Charles Crabbin Project Liberty Ship	Box 8 Long Green, MD 21092	(301) 661–1550
USS *North Carolina*	USS *North Carolina* Battleship Memorial	Box 417 Wilmington, NC 28402	(919) 762–1829
USS *Yorktown* USS *Laffey* USS *Clamagore* USCGC *Ingham*	Patriots Point Museum	40 Patriots Point Road Mount Pleasant, SC 29464	(803) 884–2727
USS *Alabama* USS *Drum*	USS *Alabama* Battleship Commission	Box 65 Mobile, AL 36601	(205) 433–2703
USS *Kidd*	USS *Kidd* and Nautical Historic Center	305 South River Road Baton Rouge, LA 70802	(504) 342–1942
USS *Texas*	Battleship Texas	3527 Battleground Road La Porte, TX 77571	(713) 479–2411
USS *Stewart* USS *Cavalla*	Seawolf Park Moody Civic Center	21st Street and Beach Boulevard Galveston, TX 77550	(713) 744–5738
USS *Cod*	Naval Reserve Center	1089 East 9th Street Cleveland, OH 44114	(216) 566–8770
USS *Silversides*	USS *Silversides* Maritime Museum	Box 1692 Muskegon, MI 49443	(616) 744–9117
USS *Cobia*	Manitowoc Maritime Museum	75 Maritime Drive Manitowoc, WI 54220-6843	(414) 684–0218
USS *Hazard*	Freedom Park	2497 Freedom Park Road Omaha, NE 68110	(402) 345–1959

The *Texas* under a full head of steam

Youthful imaginations bring history to life.

Ship	Organization	Address	Telephone
USS *Batfish*	USS *Batfish* Submarine and Military Museum	Box 253 Muskogee, OK 74401	(918) 682–6294
USS *Pampanito*	National Maritime Museum Association	Presidio of San Francisco Building 275 Crissy Field San Francisco, CA 94129	(415) 929–0202
SS *Jeremiah O'Brien*	Liberty Ship Memorial	Fort Mason Center San Francisco, CA 94123-1382	(415) 441–5705
USS *Arizona*	The Visitor Center	1 Arizona Memorial Place Honolulu, HI 96818	(808) 422–0561
USS *Bowfin*	USS *Bowfin*	11 Arizona Memorial Drive Honolulu, HI 96818	(808) 423–1341

Some battleships of World War II vintage have been recalled to active duty and continue to serve even today. Here, sailing past the supply ship *White Plains*, the USS *Wisconsin* patrols the Persian Gulf.

Photography Credits

The authors extend their appreciation to those individuals
and organizations listed below.

2 *(top)*	National Archives
2 *(bottom)*	National Archives
3	Naval Historical Center
12	Naval Historical Center
13	Robin R. Renken, Major, USMC
14 *(top)*	Naval Historical Center
14 *(bottom)*	National Archives
21	National Archives
22	National Archives
29	National Archives
30	Admiral Nimitz and Naval Historical Center
31	National Archives
32	National Archives
33	National Archives
34	National Archives
64	National Archives
65	Naval Historical Center
66	Naval Historical Center
71	National Archives
72	Naval Historical Center
89	Naval Historical Center
90-91	National Archives
92	Naval Historical Center
99	Naval Historical Center
103	National Archives
110-11	Naval Historical Center
112-13	National Archives
129	Naval Historical Center
130-31	Robin R. Renken, Major, USMC
132	Robin R. Renken, Major, USMC
135	National Archives
140	National Archives
142-43	National Archives
146-47	Reuters/Bettmann

About the Authors

The award-winning photographs of Bruce Roberts, a senior photographer for *Southern Living* magazine, have appeared in *Life, Sports Illustrated,* Time-Life Books, and other publications.

Ray Jones, a freelance writer, has written for Time-Life Books as well as *Albuquerque Living* and *Southern Living* magazines.